Why Airplanes Crash

Why Airplanes Crash

Aviation Safety
in a Changing World

CLINTON V. OSTER, JR.

JOHN S. STRONG

C. KURT ZORN

New York   Oxford
OXFORD UNIVERSITY PRESS
1992

Oxford University Press

Oxford   New York   Toronto
Delhi   Bombay   Calcutta   Madras   Karachi
Kuala Lumpur   Singapore   Hong Kong   Tokyo
Nairobi   Dar es Salaam   Cape Town
Melbourne   Auckland

and associated companies in
Berlin   Ibadan

Copyright © 1992 by Oxford University Press, Inc.

Published by Oxford University Press, Inc.
200 Madison Avenue, New York, New York 10016

Library of Congress Cataloging-in-Publication Data
Oster, Clinton V., Jr.
Why airplanes crash: aviation safety in a changing world
Clinton V. Oster, Jr., John S. Strong, C. Kurt Zorn
p. cm.   Includes Index
ISBN 0-19-507223-5
1. Aeronautics—Accidents.
2. Aeronautics—United States—Accidents.
3. Aeronautics—Canada—Accidents.
I. Strong, John S. II. Zorn, C. Kurt. III. Title
TL553.5.O73   1992   363.12'41—dc20
91-33818

1 3 5 7 9 8 6 4 2

Printed in the United States of America
on acid-free paper

We dedicate this book to John R. Meyer of Harvard University — scholar, professor, mentor, colleague, and valued friend. For many years, his example and encouragement have prompted us to think deeply about the many issues in the relationship between business and government.

Preface

This book has its roots in two research projects that involved the three authors. The Harvard Airline Deregulation Study, which began in 1979, resulted in three books on the airline industry. During this research, questions about effects of deregulation on safety were raised, in particular the safety performance of commuter airlines and new entrant carriers. The second project involved participation in the President's Commission on Aviation Safety, which was established in 1987 to provide a comprehensive study of U.S. airline safety. Clinton Oster served as research director for the Commission, and John Strong and C. Kurt Zorn served as consultants to the study. The Commission's April 1988 report provided a review of many of the public policy issues concerning airline safety and issued recommendations, many of which are in place today. Much of the research and analysis presented in this book was begun during that time. The authors would like to acknowledge the many participants in that effort; we hope that many of their ideas and concerns are represented in this book.

Parts of this book are related to other research or projects undertaken by the authors. Much of the analysis of the Canadian air safety record is based on work done by Clinton Oster as part of a project conducted by Sypher: Mueller International. Parts of the analysis of international air safety are related to John Strong's work with Garuda Indonesia Airlines, under contract through the Harvard Institute for International Development. The Transportation Research Board of the National Academy of Sciences Study of Air Passenger Service and Safety Since Deregulation, on which Oster served as a commission member and Strong as a consultant, was helpful in clarifying and sharpening many of the issues raised here.

This book would not have been possible without the extensive help of many people in the aviation community. In particular we would like to thank Stan Smith of the National Transportation Safety Board in Washington, D.C., for his many efforts in helping us obtain, understand, and analyze the vast amount of aviation accident data. Olof Fritsch of the International Civil Aviation Organization was very helpful in guiding us through international aviation data. Gerry Cohen, Tom Richardson, Cal Watson, Earl Weener and Peter Wheeler of Boeing provided valuable assistance, ideas, and information. Also helpful were discussions with Peter Potocki de Montalk of Airbus Industrie; Michel Pacull, Hugues Subra de Salafa, and Jacques Troyes of Aerospatiale; Desmond Charles, Chris Davies, Ted Talbot, and Roger Taplin of British Aerospace; and Derrell Brown, Max Klotzsche, Mike Newman, and David Swain of McDonnell-Douglas. Jim Landry of the Air Transport Association in Washington helped provide industry data and helpful comments.

Many persons reviewed all or part of the manuscript, provided comments, and suggested improvements that have contributed to the final version. In particular we would like to acknowledge Ben Berman of the National Transportation Safety Board; Steve Godwin of the Transportation Research Board; Richard Golaszewski of Gellman Research Associates; Michael Levine of Yale; Jim Marr of MIT; John R. Meyer of Harvard; Don Pickrell of the U.S. Department of Transportation; Nancy Rose of MIT; and Gordon Hamilton, Robin Monroe, and David Biggs of Sypher:Mueller International. Herb Addison of Oxford University Press and the anonymous referees who reviewed our manuscript also are due many thanks.

Several institutions and individuals provided research and technical support. At Indiana University, the Transportation Research Center of the School of Public and Environmental Affairs and the School of Business provided a base for the project. Darrell Spears of the Indiana University Computer Center was essential in helping prepare and analyze data. Donna McLean and Paula Wendell provided excellent research assistance. Heather Ratliff was helpful on general aviation topics in the later stages of the project. Steffanie Curry and Cheryl Picou managed to keep track of many drafts and keep the production of the book running smoothly. Cynthia Mahigian Moorhead provided able assistance in the production of camera-ready copy of the final manuscript.

The School of Business Administration of The College of William and Mary provided ongoing research support for John Strong. The Thomas Jefferson Program in Public Policy at William and Mary participated in the effort through its sponsorship of a conference on the airline industry in November 1990. Carole Chappell, Melissa Reagan, Nancy Smith and Phyllis Viands provided cheerful staff support. During the fall of 1989, the Center for Business and Government at the Kennedy School of Government, Harvard University provided research support for John Strong, much of which was devoted to aviation safety.

We would like to thank our wives Christine, Carol, and Lisa, and our children Heather, Graham, Kala, and Kersten for their support and perseverance through years of research, travel, and countless discussion on airlines and aviation safety.

Finally, of course the conclusions and opinions are those of the authors and do not necessarily reflect those of individuals or institutions that have provided us with support or assistance.

Bloomington, Ind   C. V. O., Jr.

Williamsburg, Va.   J. S. S.

Bloomington, Ind.   C. K. Z.

November, 1991

Contents

Tables and Figures

Figures

Why Airplanes Crash

Chapter 1

Risk in Air Travel

A series of well-publicized aviation accidents and dramatic changes in airline industry structure during the 1980s and early 1990s have fueled growing public concern about safety. The horrific consequences of a major airline accident have been brought to the public's attention in dramatic fashion by accidents such as the 1982 crashes of Air Florida in Washington, D.C., and Pan Am in a New Orleans suburb; the 1985 crashes of Delta Airlines in Dallas-Fort Worth and Midwest Express in Milwaukee; the 1986 collision over Los Angeles between an Aeromexico passenger jet and a general aviation aircraft; the 1987 accidents in Detroit and Denver involving Northwest Airlines and Continental Airlines, respectively; the 1988 bombing of a Pan Am B-747 over Lockerbie, Scotland; the crash landing of a United Airlines DC-10 in Sioux City in 1989; the runway collisions between two Northwest jets in 1990 and between a USAir B-737 and a Skywest commuter plane in 1991; and the 1991 crash of a United B-737 in Colorado Springs. While crashes of smaller commuter aircraft and private planes generally receive less attention than those of large airliners, even these accidents have received somewhat greater publicity than in the past because of the recent deaths of well-known sports, entertainment, and political figures.

While the media has made the traveling and nontraveling public alike aware of the potential dangers of air travel, the growing concern with safety extends beyond the public and the media to the aviation industry and government officials. Some industry observers contend the number and severity of airline accidents only scratch the surface; an even more serious problem in aviation is a deterioration in the underlying safety of the industry. These observers point to reports of increased numbers of near midair collisions, increased errors by overworked air traffic controllers, large fines levied against airlines for maintenance violations and falsified maintenance records, and other incidents as supporting evidence. Some critics claim airline deregulation is at fault and the solution is to re-regulate the industry.[1] Others contend the fault lies with the government's regulatory agency, the Federal Aviation Administration (FAA), and not with deregulation. These observers believe the FAA is ill-equipped to ensure safety in a dynamic deregulated airline industry and their solution is to restructure the government's approach to safety.[2]

This book is about aviation safety and why airplanes crash. It begins by examining the safety record of the U.S. jet and commuter airline industry, but it goes beyond that to address broader concerns. Has deregulation reduced the safety of the U.S. airline industry? Has airline maintenance suffered under deregulation's competitive pressures with a resulting increase in equipment failures? Have greater demands on the air traffic control system reduced the system's safety? Does the growing use of commuter airlines pose a safety threat to the traveling public?

As important as these questions are, scheduled airline service accounts for only about 12 percent of U.S. aviation fatalities. In order to provide a more complete picture, this book also examines the safety record and the reasons for accidents in the nonscheduled and general aviation segments of the industry, where the bulk of U.S. fatalities occur and where airline pilots increasingly receive most of their training and experience.

The recent boom in international air travel has helped bring people throughout the world closer together. Aviation accidents are worldwide phenomena; some of the worst air disasters have occurred outside the United States. This book examines aviation safety throughout the world, first with a comparison of Canadian and U.S. aviation safety, and then with a look at air safety in all regions of the world. Two emerging issues will then be examined in greater detail: aging aircraft and terrorism.

MAJOR CONCLUSIONS

Several important findings emerge from this study. An overview

---

[1]John J. Nance, "Economic Deregulation's Unintended but Inevitable Impact on Airline Safety," in Leon Moses and Ian Savage, editors, *Transportation Safety in an Age of Deregulation* (New York: Oxford University Press, 1989).

[2]Aviation Safety Commission, *Volume I: Final Report and Recommendations* (Washington, D.C.: Government Printing Office, April 1988).

of the U.S. airline safety record for the 1970-1989 period shows that the rates at which passengers have been killed or seriously injured on jet carriers generally have followed a downward trend (Figure 1.1). There is no evidence that deregulation has resulted in a worsening safety record or that the air traffic control system has been thus far unable to cope with post-deregulation growth. Not only has the airline safety record been better in the years following deregulation than it was before, but the rates of accidents caused by equipment failure, air traffic control error, and pilot error have all dropped. Similarly, the accident rates for commuter airlines also have shown a downward trend throughout the period (Figure 1.2). Indeed, the commuter industry's safety has improved to the point that in the late 1980s the safety performance of the largest commuters equaled that of the jet carriers. In the 1977-1989 period, the odds of dying on a U.S. domestic scheduled airline flight had fallen to less than 1 in 2 million.

Jet carrier accident rates for fatal, serious, and minor accidents also have shown a downward trend (Figure 1.3), but the safety record has varied substantially from year to year, making it difficult to detect changing trends in safety. Because accidents are in some sense the outcome of increases in the risk of flying, many travelers and industry personnel worry that an increase in accidents over the previous year might be an early sign of a long-run deterioration in safety. While there is an understandable temptation to draw conclusions from year-to-year changes in

Figure 1.1 U.S. Jet Airlines, Fatalities and Serious Injuries, 1970-1989

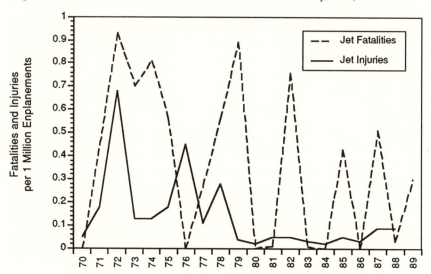

Figure 1.2 U.S. Commuter Airlines, Fatalities and Serious Injuries, 1970-1989

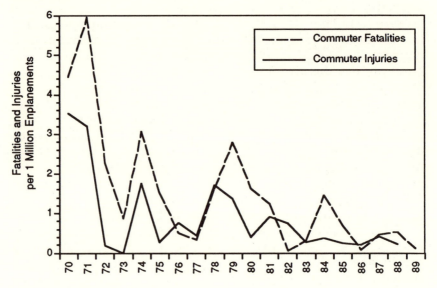

Figure 1.3 U.S. Airline Safety Jet, Carrier Accidents, 1970-1989

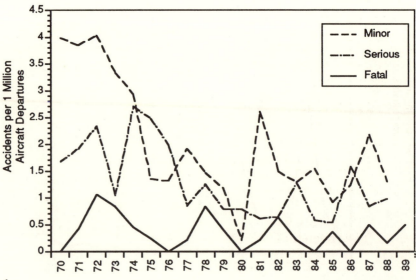

6

overall safety rates, aviation safety is a complex topic that demands a more thorough analysis.

When the safety record of U.S. scheduled airlines is considered along with the records of nonscheduled airlines and general aviation, a picture of "risk tiers" emerges. As one moves from general aviation to charters or air taxis to scheduled commuters to scheduled jet airlines, safety generally improves and pilot error plays a smaller role in accidents. These risk tiers mirror the career progression of many pilots. The irony is that as pilots become more experienced and as less capable pilots are filtered out in the hiring process, these better pilots fly more capable equipment with greater reliability and more backup systems. Thus, there is a "safety mismatch" where the least experienced pilots are flying the least capable aircraft. A similar pattern of risk tiers is found in Canada.

Risk tiers also emerge when worldwide aviation is examined. Here, the risk tiers are amplified by the historic practice of selling used aircraft to the developing world. While there are some important exceptions, airlines in developing countries are found to have dramatically less safe operations. Many of these airlines are flying older aircraft containing outdated technology that have been passed down from service in the developed world. Older aircraft require more extensive maintenance with more sophisticated inspection techniques to ensure their structural integrity. The trickle down practice of passing aircraft to the developing world has the effect of putting the oldest aircraft in service in the world's most difficult operating environments and in the hands of the people perhaps less able to maintain the aircraft. Moreover, pilots in these countries often do not have the benefit of the latest technology training simulators or crew training techniques. Compounding these problems is the increasingly sophisticated threat of terrorism and sabotage.

PROFILE OF A FLIGHT

To understand these conclusions and to place them in the proper context, it is helpful to examine the nature of risk in air travel by following a typical flight to see both the potential dangers in various portions of the flight and how the U.S. air traffic control system operates. From the passengers' perspective, the flight begins with a walk down the jetway to the aircraft. Precautions already have been taken to enhance passenger safety. Passengers and their carry-on luggage have been screened by airport security in an attempt to detect any weapons, explosives, or other hazardous materials. Checked luggage may have also been examined for explosives. In some cases, passengers may have been checked against profiles thought to reflect the characteristics of terrorists or those likely to be the unwitting carriers of terrorist bombs. On international flights by U.S. carriers, additional steps have been taken to insure that no baggage has been loaded on the plane unless the passenger who checked the baggage actually has boarded the flight. Prior to making final preparations for departure the pilot or another member of the flight crew will have made a "walk around" inspection of the aircraft to check for visible problems with landing gear, engines, and the like.

Once all passengers, baggage, and cargo are loaded and the aircraft has been fueled and serviced, the pilot requests permission and instructions from the air traffic controller in the airport tower to "push back" from the gate and taxi to the appropriate runway for takeoff. Clearance to leave the gate and taxi to the runway for takeoff may not be given to the aircraft right away. If more aircraft are bound for an airport at a particular time than that airport can accommodate, the Central Flow Control Facility of the air traffic control system may instruct the aircraft to "hold" on the ground to reduce the flow of aircraft to a congested airport to a level that can be accommodated without airborne delay. The FAA, which operates the air traffic control system, intentionally holds aircraft on the ground at the origin airport rather than have the aircraft circling in the air at the destination airport. This practice is not only safer than the earlier practice of having aircraft circle the destination airport until it was their turn to land, it reduces fuel consumption as well.

Little risk is associated with the initial phase of flight involving passenger loading, leaving the gate, and taxiing. Only 2.7 percent of fatal accidents occur during loading, unloading, and taxi. Passengers occasionally do fall from jetways and emergencies at the gate can lead to evacuations that result in passenger injuries. More common are collisions between taxiing aircraft and parked aircraft or between aircraft and ground vehicles, but these accidents are rarely fatal to passengers. A more serious threat to passenger safety during taxiing is the potential high-speed collision between a taxiing aircraft and an aircraft taking off or landing. In 1977 in Tenerife, for example, 583 people were killed when a KLM B-747 on a takeoff roll collided with a Pan Am B-747 taxiing to the terminal following landing. In 1990, a Northwest Airlines jet in Detroit became disoriented while taxiing in fog and mistakenly taxied onto an active runway where it collided with a departing

Northwest jet. Eight people were killed and twenty-one were seriously injured.

Once an aircraft has taxied to the runway it will receive instructions from the controller in the tower to "taxi into position and hold," which means to position the aircraft on the runway ready for takeoff, and then be informed that it is "clear for takeoff." At many airports, the controller giving taxi instructions will be different from the controller giving takeoff instructions, although both will be operating from the same tower and working in close coordination. A potential safety problem can arise at this point. During slower periods, an aircraft is told to taxi into position and hold; once in position, takeoff clearance is given right away. If multiple runways and taxiways are being used however, a plane may be requested to taxi into position and hold for takeoff clearance even though the runway may have active or crossing traffic. In this situation, two planes could occupy the same runway at the same time. In Los Angeles in 1991, a Skywest commuter plane was holding for takeoff when a USAir B-737 landed on the same runway, killing all aboard the smaller plane. Once an aircraft has taken off and begun its initial climb, the pilot will be instructed to contact a different air traffic controller in "Departure Control" on a different radio frequency. Departure Control is part of the operation in the Terminal Radar Approach Control (TRACON). The TRACON is responsible for controlling aircraft during arrival and departure in the vicinity of the airport.

Takeoff and initial climb, that portion of the climb prior to the retraction of the aircraft's flaps and landing gear, are probably, minute for minute, the most hazardous portions of flight.[3] Together they account for only 2 percent of flight time yet nearly 23 percent of fatal accidents occur in these phases of flight. Mechanical failures or malfunctions pose a particularly serious hazard when the aircraft is moving quickly on the ground or flying close to the ground. The flight crew has little time to react to problems and the aircraft may be sluggish to respond to controls because of the weight of a full fuel load coupled with relatively low airspeed.

The 1987 crashes in Detroit and Denver, the 1985 crash in Milwaukee, and the 1982 crashes in Washington and New Orleans illustrate the kinds of problems that can occur during takeoff and initial climb. In Detroit, a Northwest Airlines MD-80 crashed on takeoff when the flight crew failed to extend the flaps to the proper position. In Denver, a Continental Airlines DC-9 crashed on takeoff in adverse weather conditions through what appears

[3]The flaps are the retractable extensions to the aircraft's wings that, when extended, give the wings extra lift at low speeds.

to have been a combination of bad weather, difficult winds, and pilot error. In Milwaukee, a Midwest Express DC-9 suffered an engine failure on takeoff. In Washington, an Air Florida B-737 crashed on takeoff due to a combination of ice accumulation on the aircraft and pilot error. In New Orleans, a Pan American B-727 crashed on takeoff when it encountered windshear.[4]

As the aircraft approaches the boundary of the terminal radar control area, it is "handed off" to an Air Route Traffic Control Center (ARTCC or "Center") and told to contact the Center controller on a different radio frequency. There are twenty ARTCCs in the continental United States, with each responsible for handling en route traffic passing through a specific geographic area between airport terminal areas. Each Center's area is further divided into specific blocks of airspace called sectors with each sector typically handled by two, but in some instances up to four, controllers. As the aircraft continues along its route, it is handed off from sector to sector within each Center and from Center to Center across the country. These hand-offs are accomplished with the aid of computer-based communication. The task of the ARTCC controllers is to maintain sufficient separation between aircraft under their control, to be sure that the aircraft maintain the correct altitude and direction, and to make sure the aircraft enter the terminal airspace at their destination at the proper altitude, speed, and with proper spacing between aircraft so that the TRACON can take over and guide them to a safe landing.

The climb, cruise, and initial descent phases of flight are substantially less risky than are the takeoff and initial climb. In a typical flight the climb phase accounts for 13 percent of flight time and 8.4 percent of fatal accidents; cruise accounts for 60 percent of flight time and 7.7 percent of fatal accidents; descent is somewhat riskier accounting for 10 percent of flight time and 12.8 percent of fatal accidents. While mechanical failures can occur in these phases of flight, the higher altitudes at which the aircraft are operating give the flight crew more time to react and recover.

Higher altitude, however, is not always an asset in an emergency. In 1983, an Air Canada flight from Dallas to Toronto

[4]Windshear is a weather phenomenon where a column of air descends rapidly and vertically to the ground where it fans out in a pattern similar to an inverted mushroom. An aircraft flying into and through windshear first encounters a strong headwind, which in itself poses no particular problem. The aircraft then encounters a strong downdraft pushing it toward the ground followed by a sudden strong tailwind that causes the aircraft to lose airspeed, which in turn causes a loss of lift causing the aircraft to descend still further to the ground. If the windshear is only moderate and if the pilot recognizes it immediately and responds properly, the aircraft may recover prior to impact with the ground. If strong windshear is encountered, recovery is not possible no matter what actions the pilot takes.

had a fire break out in the rear lavatory while in cruise. By the time an emergency descent, landing, and evacuation in Cincinnati was made, the fire had progressed to the point that twenty-three of the forty-one passengers lost their lives. Similarly, added time for the crew to react to a mechanical problem may not be enough to prevent an accident if the problem is sufficiently severe. In 1989, a United Airlines DC-10 suffered an engine failure where part of the engine left the engine compartment, penetrated the fuselage and severed the hydraulic lines, eliminating most of the pilot's means of controlling the aircraft. The plane subsequently crashed during an attempted emergency landing in Sioux City, Iowa, killing 112 people.

Bombs placed aboard the aircraft may also explode during the cruise portion of flight. In 1985, an Air India B-747 exploded in flight while over the Atlantic Ocean from a bomb in the cargo hold. In 1988, a Pan Am B-747 exploded over Scotland from a bomb in the luggage compartment. These two crashes alone killed 599 people. Structural failures also can occur during cruise. In April 1988, a large portion of the top half of the fuselage of an Aloha Airlines B-737 was torn off in flight. Remarkably, the aircraft landed safely and only one person died.

Virtually all commercial airline flights operate under instrument flight rules (IFR) and participate in the air traffic control system under what is known as "positive control," where the aircraft are under the explicit direction of air traffic controllers. The computer system used by air traffic control has the aircraft's flight plan, which had been filed with and approved by the air traffic control system prior to the flight. These aircraft are equipped with transponders. Transponders are electronic devices that send information to the air traffic control system radar about the identity of the aircraft. Transponders in airliners have "Mode C" capability, which includes the altitude of the aircraft as part of the information sent to air traffic control.

In good weather, there are also small private general aviation aircraft flying in specific areas under visual flight rules (VFR) who are not participating in the air traffic control system and are considered "uncontrolled" aircraft. These other aircraft may or may not have transponders and those with transponders may or may not have Mode C capability. Uncontrolled general aviation aircraft are the principal source of midair collision risk for passenger airliners. Midair collisions are possible in all phases of flight, but they are more likely to occur at lower altitudes where airspace is shared by both VFR and IFR traffic and where responsibility to avoid collisions rests with the pilots. In 1991, a Southwest

Airlines B-737 missed an unidentified general aviation aircraft by 50 feet on approach to Midway Airport in Chicago. The smaller plane was not equipped with a Mode C transponder. Since the cruise stage of flight is generally at high altitude, midair collisions during cruise are quite rare. Even so, there is some risk of midair collision in cruise. In 1981, an Air U.S. commuter flight was in cruise over Loveland, Colorado, when it collided with a general aviation plane carrying skydivers. All of the commuter passengers were killed.

The air traffic control computer system assembles information from multiple radar sites, combines it with flight plans, and displays each aircraft as a symbol on the screen of a controller's plan view display (PVD). To the controller, the scheduled airliner appears as a symbol with an attached "data block" that tells the controller the air carrier and flight number, the type of aircraft, the aircraft's altitude and airspeed, and its destination airport.

The controller's screen also shows other symbols without data blocks which move across the display. These symbols usually represent uncontrolled VFR aircraft. On occasion, the marked symbols representing controlled traffic appear to approach and even merge with unmarked symbols on the screen. While the convergence of these symbols might indicate imminent collision, this generally is not the case. The aircraft represented by unmarked symbols are supposed to be (and almost always are) at different altitudes than the airliners represented by the marked symbols. However, if a general aviation aircraft does not have or is not using a Mode C transponder, the air traffic controller has no way of knowing for sure.

In clear weather, the pilots of both controlled and uncontrolled aircraft have the responsibility to watch out for other traffic and maintain separation. Depending upon where they are flying, aircraft must maintain at least three to five miles horizontal separation and 1000 feet vertical separation. If air traffic control workload permits, controllers try to warn controlled aircraft about uncontrolled aircraft observed on radar that may pose a threat of collision. This warning would result in the receiving aircraft pilot immediately beginning a visual search for the other aircraft. When the uncontrolled aircraft has a Mode C transponder the controller would provide a "callout" indicating the traffic's position and altitude.

A plus or circle radar symbol is generated by an aircraft equipped with a transponder but no encoding altimeter—without Mode C. The controller knows the plane's approximate location, but not its altitude. Using this information, the controller can issue traffic advisories to controlled aircraft that include the relative horizontal position of the uncontrolled aircraft, but not its altitude. The uncontrolled aircraft may be an immediate threat or it may be several thousand feet above or below the controlled aircraft; the controller has no way of knowing. If the uncontrolled aircraft is following the correct procedures, as is almost always the case, there is no threat of collision because the aircraft is not supposed to be at the same altitude as the controlled aircraft. In this situation, the controller may issue the advisory as "altitude unknown," but if the controller is very busy, there may not be any advisory issued.

Some of the radar symbols (in particular, squares or asterisks) can be safely ignored by a busy controller. These radar symbols are generated by aircraft equipped with Mode C transponders that are not operating at an altitude for which the controller is responsible. They have been "filtered" by the air traffic control computer, and the symbol tells the controller that the traffic is either above or below the airspace which is that particular controller's responsibility and, consequently, the indicated VFR traffic is not in potential conflict with any of the controller's aircraft.

The controller's screen also shows vague smudges, which are generated by aircraft without any transponder equipment. They are the "primary" radar reflections from the aircraft's metal skin or they might have been generated by rain showers. Although they may represent some safety risk, a controller does not have enough information to provide useful traffic advisories or separation. Some smudges may also indicate objects on the ground that are mistakenly picked up by radar. For example, in some types of terrain, it is not unusual for air traffic control radar to track large trucks moving on nearby highways. In addition, controllers know that the symbols appearing in their screens may not represent all of the uncontrolled aircraft. Because of blind spots and other characteristics of radars, some aircraft (especially those that do not have transponders) may appear only sporadically on the screen or may not appear at all.

As the flight nears its destination airport, it is handed off to a controller working an "Approach Control" position in the TRACON. During the initial approach phase of flight, several streams of traffic inbound from different directions will be merged into a single stream aligned for the landing runway. This process is quite similar to merging onto a highway. As the aircraft begins its final approach to the airport, it is handed off to a controller in the airport tower for the final approach and landing. It is then handed off again, this time to a ground controller for taxi to the arrival gate.

Initial approach, final approach, and landing are relatively hazardous phases of flight. Initial approach accounts for 11 percent of flight time but for 16.2 percent of fatal accidents. Final approach accounts for only 3 percent of flight time but for 24.2 percent of fatal accidents. Landing accounts for 1 percent of flight time but for 5.1 percent of fatal accidents. As with takeoff and initial climb, the aircraft is close to the ground in these phases of flight, leaving the flight crew with little time to react to mechanical or weather problems. Moreover, these aircraft are now at altitudes where uncontrolled general aviation aircraft are capable of operating.

Many examples illustrate the hazards associated with these phases. In 1982, a World Airways DC-10 slid off the end of the runway while landing in Boston, killing two passengers. In 1985, a Delta Airlines flight crashed on approach to Dallas when it encountered windshear, killing 126 passengers. In 1986, an Aeromexico jetliner collided in midair with a general aviation aircraft over Los Angeles, demonstrating the possible consequences of uncontrolled aircraft straying into controlled airspace. The 1991 collision in Los Angeles between a USAir jet and a Skywest commuter mentioned earlier occurred while the USAir plane was landing.

Finally, the aircraft taxis to the gate where the passengers deplane and the baggage and cargo are unloaded. These portions of the flight are relatively safe, although in 1985 a bomb exploded while baggage was being unloaded from an American Airlines plane at Dallas-Ft. Worth. Fortunately, no one was killed. Other potential safety problems during this time involve ground equipment and airport vehicles interfering with the traffic patterns of airplanes on the taxiways and gate aprons.

While there is risk associated with all portions of flight, it is important to remember that the overwhelming majority of flights are safe and uneventful. Indeed, it is the uneventful nature of most flights that brings so much attention to these few flights where something goes wrong.

OVERVIEW OF THE BOOK

To improve airline safety, one must begin by asking why airplanes crash and, in particular, why airplanes in some segments of the industry seem to crash more frequently than in other segments.

In Chapter 2, the jet carrier and commuter carrier segments of the industry are examined in detail in the both the pre- and post-deregulation periods. While the general conclusion is that safety has been better in the post-deregulation period than it had been before, a close examination raises some potentially troubling issues. For example, in the most recent years, commuters have continued to improve their safety, but jet carriers have not. Indeed, in the 1986-1988 period, jet carriers crashed slightly more often from pilot error and equipment failure than they did in the years immediately following deregulation. Is this an indication of the risk of keeping aircraft in service longer and rapidly expanding the pilot work force, or is it merely another example of the year-to-year variation that can make safety analysis so difficult?

Chapter 3 turns to the rest of the U.S. aviation industry: jet charter operators, air taxi operators, cargo carriers, and general aviation. All of these segments of the industry have generally worse safety records than do their scheduled counterparts, and general aviation kills far more people in the United States than do jet and commuter carriers combined. For the 1987-1989 period, for each person killed in scheduled jet carrier service, eight were killed in general aviation accidents. Beyond being a source of concern in their own right, these segments of the industry are the training ground for the pilots who will eventually fly for the scheduled jet and commuter airlines. Indeed, comparing these industry segments with those in Chapter 2 poses the paradoxical mismatch that in the United States, the least experienced pilots are gaining experience by flying the least sophisticated aircraft in some of the most difficult flight environments.

Chapter 4 begins to place the U.S. experience in an international context by comparing it with the Canadian safety record. Although facing a similar flight environment, large Canadian jet carriers appear to have a worse safety record than do their U.S. counterparts. However, Canadian commuter carriers appear to have safety records similar to those of their closest U.S. counterparts. What causes these differences between the U.S. and Canadian carriers? To provide an appropriate basis for comparison with Canadian carriers, U.S. carriers operating in Alaska are contrasted with those in the lower 48 states. Here again, systematic differences in safety performance are found.

Chapter 5 places the North American experience in a global context by examining airline safety throughout the world. Airline safety performance is found to vary widely and systematically across regions of the world and among carriers within these regions. These differences, some of which are dramatic and troubling, are of increasing interest and concern in an emerging era of mergers, financial linkages, and marketing agreements among international airlines.

Chapter 6 addresses the concern that an analysis of accidents cannot provide early warning of deteriorating safety. The so-called margin of safety is examined as are a series of possible nonaccident indicators of safety. Questions addressed include whether such events as near midair collisions, air traffic control errors, runway incursions, or deteriorating financial conditions of airlines can be interpreted as precursors of increased accidents.

Chapter 7 addresses the specific concerns posed by the aging of the worldwide aircraft fleet. In most people's minds, the aging aircraft issue recalls the vivid image of the Aloha Airlines plane landing with a substantial portion of its fuselage missing. The issue, of course, goes beyond that one incident to a problem of growing concern not only in the United States, but throughout the world.

Chapter 8 turns to the issue of the threats to aviation safety posed by terrorism and sabotage. These are not new threats, but their character has changed markedly in recent years. While the means of combating hijacking and sabotage have grown more sophisticated, so have the tools available to hijackers and terrorists. It is a technological race that the aviation industry may not be able to win.

Chapter 9 focuses on the themes and policy issues that arise from the analysis of safety presented in the previous chapters. It highlights important conclusions, focusing on the major challenges to continued improvements in aviation safety. The foundation upon which these conclusions are built begins in the next chapter with an examination of U.S. airline safety in an era of deregulation.

I

THE SAFETY RECORD

Chapter 2

The U.S. Airline Safety Record in the Post-Deregulation Era

The U.S. airline industry has changed dramatically since passage of the Airline Deregulation Act in 1978. Flexibility in route entry and exit and in fare setting stimulated competition, encouraged new entrants, and forced all airlines to pay more attention to cost control, productivity improvements, and marketing. These changes, while generally beneficial for consumers,[1] have raised questions and concern about safety. While the early post-deregulation years were characterized by rapid industry growth and the creation of many new airlines, the years following 1986 have been characterized by industry consolidation and serious financial problems among several large carriers. Even though safety regulation was not directly affected by the Airline Deregulation Act of 1978[2] some participants and observers of the industry fear that there has been an unintended negative impact.

---

[1] John R. Meyer and Clinton V. Oster, Jr., *Deregulation and the Future of Intercity Passenger Travel* (Cambridge: The MIT Press, 1987), pp. 83-107.

[2] Commuter safety regulations were tightened in 1978, the same year the Deregulation Act was passed, but these safety changes had been in the works for several years and it was coincidental that both happened the same year.

DEREGULATION'S POTENTIAL IMPACTS ON SAFETY

Many who are concerned about deregulation's potentially adverse impact on safety contend that fare competition has weakened the financial status of many carriers, forcing them to reduce expenditures in critically important areas. Specifically, many carriers are alleged to have reduced their pilot training and maintenance activities to the minimum required by FAA regulations as they focus on maintaining short-run profitability and generating a positive cash flow. Several carriers have been assessed high fines by the FAA for maintenance practices that did not meet FAA standards.[3] Reductions in maintenance expenditures and maintenance personnel are offered as evidence of safety degradation resulting from these financial pressures. Perhaps most ominously, in early 1991 Eastern Airlines agreed to pay a $3.5 million fine and pleaded guilty to falsifying maintenance records to cover up its failure to do required maintenance.

Airline industry expansion and the wave of mergers and acquisitions since 1986 have had two principal effects on carrier financial performance. First, an already highly leveraged industry has become more leveraged in the wake of massive equipment purchases and acquisition-related debt. The airline industry has never been a stellar financial performer; only once in the first forty years of the post-World War II period, in 1984, did the airline industry return on investment exceed that for all nonfinancial corporations. Airline stock indices have underperformed both the market and other transportation sectors throughout the deregulated period, except for the run up in airline stock prices during the merger activity during 1987 and 1989.[4]

Second, the distribution of industry profits and losses has changed. In the regulated era, route awards and standardized pricing meant that size and profitability across carriers were much more even. In the 1980s, and early 1990s though, there has been a growing divergence in financial performance. A few major airlines have experienced persistent losses while others have either maintained profitability or have shown swings between income and losses.[5] Each of these developments has raised new concerns about the airlines' ability to maintain safe operations.

The sharp increase in traffic volume stimulated in part by lower fares in the post-deregulation era has placed considerable pressure on the airlines to offer more flights. Expansion has

[3]"FAA Points Finger at Airline Maintenance Systems," *Air Transport World*, February 1987, pp. 62-68.
[4]Meyer and Oster, *Deregulation and the Future of Intercity Passenger Travel*, p. 19.
[5]*Ibid.*, pp. 17-38.

required the rapid hiring of new pilots, raising concern about both the experience levels of pilots and possibly less stringent hiring standards. Expansion has also placed pressure on aircraft manufacturers to increase production and on airlines to keep older aircraft in service longer.

Deregulation has been claimed to have degraded safety through its liberalization of route entry and exit. New carriers could more easily begin operations following deregulation resulting in an influx of new entrant jet carriers in the early 1980s that some have argued had a negative effect on safety.[6] In addition, commuter airlines flying small turboprop aircraft have replaced large jet airlines on many routes, especially in small community service. Commuter carriers are perceived to be dramatically less safe than are large jet airlines.

Deregulation's route freedoms have allowed airlines to exploit the service advantages of hub and spoke route systems. By having a group of aircraft from many destinations all converge at an airport at about the same time, a great many connecting opportunities then can be offered passengers. If too many flights converge at one time, however, airport and airspace capacity can be strained, with congestion-related delays, declines in service quality, and much greater pressure on air traffic control to keep aircraft from colliding in the air or on the ground.

In addition to the impacts of intensified hubbing, the increase in traffic volume stimulated in part by deregulation's lower fares, coupled with the 1981 dismissal of striking Professional Air Traffic Controllers Organization (PATCO) controllers has increased pressure throughout most of the nation's air traffic control system. Fewer controllers have been asked to handle much greater volumes of traffic, raising the possibility of more air traffic control errors and a greater risk of collision.

There are clearly significant concerns about how deregulation has affected safety in the airline industry. This chapter addresses these concerns by analyzing two major issues. First, has airline safety, in the aggregate, improved or worsened in the wake of deregulation? Second, what is the evidence regarding the concerns about deregulation's impacts on specific aspects of airline safety?

SOURCES OF DATA

National Transportation Safety Board (NTSB) accident

---

[6]Arnold Barnett and Mary Higgins, "Airline Safety: The Last Decade," *Management Science* 35 (1) (January 1989):1-21.

investigations provide a rich source of accident data for scheduled, nonscheduled, and general aviation operations. These data include the number of fatalities and injuries for both passengers and crew, a description of the aircraft involved, and details concerning the circumstances surrounding the accident.

Operations data are somewhat more limited. Fairly complete data for jet carrier operations, including aircraft departures and passenger enplanements, were obtained from Civil Aeronautics Board (CAB) Form 41 and the U.S. Department of Transportation, which continued collection of these data after the sunset of the CAB. Commuter operations data were limited to passenger enplanements due to the lack of a complete and consistent source of commuter departure data. Passenger enplanements were obtained from CAB Form 298 supplemented in some years by data from the annual reports of the Regional Airline Association. For those carriers operating under Part 121[7] but classified as commuter carriers, enplanement data were obtained from CAB Form 41 and Regional Airline Association annual reports.

JET CARRIERS BEFORE AND AFTER DEREGULATION

Table 2.1 contains five measures of airline safety for combined trunk and local service airlines for both the pre-deregulation 1970-1978 period and the post-deregulation period.[8] The post-deregulation period was separated into two parts to acknowledge the differences in the industry between the 1979-1985 period and the 1986-1988 period.[9] All five safety measures show sharp improvement in the six years immediately following deregulation

[7]Federal air regulations (FAR) govern the operations of all civil aviation activities in the United States. Three major sections of those regulations govern the operations of interest in the next three chapters. Carriers operating large aircraft with more than sixty seats operate under Part 121 and are often referred to as "Part 121 Carriers." All jet carriers in the United States are in this category. Carriers operating aircraft with fewer than sixty seats operate under Part 135. Some carriers operating smaller aircraft, however, choose to operate under the more stringent Part 121 regulations. General aviation operates under Part 91, which is less stringent than Part 135.

[8]A discussion of the various measures of safety is contained in Appendix A. The trunk airlines are the descendants of the airlines originally licensed to provide interstate passenger service in 1938 and include American, Braniff, Continental, Delta, Eastern, National, Northwest, Pan American, Trans World, United, and Western. The local service airlines were originally formed to provide feeder service but evolved into regional jet carriers by the beginning of deregulation. They include USAir, Frontier, Hughes Airwest, North Central, Ozark, Piedmont, Southern, and Texas International.

[9]The distinction between trunk and local service jet carrier service is no longer relevant in the 1986-1988 period due to mergers and acquisitions. All domestic jet service, therefore, includes the trunk and local service carriers and all the carriers represented in Table 2.1 which were operating the the 1986-1988 period.

Table 2.1. Domestic Jet Carrier Service, Passenger Fatality and Aircraft Accident Rates, Domestic Scheduled Service

	Trunk and Local Service		All Domestic Jet Service
	1970-1978	1979-1985	1986-1988
Passenger Fatalities per 1 Million Enplanements	0.42	0.30	0.18[a]
Passenger Serious Injuries per 1 Million Enplanements	0.25	0.03[b]	0.07[a]
Fatal Accidents per 1 Million Aircraft Departures	0.46	0.22	0.22
Serious Injury Accidents per 1 Million Aircraft Departures	1.92	0.83	1.12
Minor Accidents per 1 Million Aircraft Departures	2.90	1.37	1.57

[a]The 1986-1988 Domestic Jet Service rate is lower than the 1970-1978 Trunk and Local Service rate at the 90 percent confidence level.
[b]The 1979-1985 Trunk and Local Service rate is lower than the 1970-1978 rate at the 95 percent confidence level.

Source: Derived from NTSB accident data; U.S. CAB, Forms 41 and 298; and Regional Airline Association, Annual Reports, various years.

and through 1988.[10] Therefore, it is hard to make the argument that deregulation has resulted in a dramatic increase in the risk associated with air travel.

Some might argue that the data contained in Table 2.1 fail to tell the complete story because two small, but important, segments of the jet carrier industry are excluded from the trunk and local service category—former intrastate and charter carriers, who increased the amount and scope of their operations after deregulation, and new entrant carriers, who appeared in the immediate post-deregulation period. Table 2.2 indicates that former intrastate and charter carriers experienced a sharp improvement in three of the five safety measures in the six years immediately following deregulation.

Due to the liberalization of route entry restrictions, many new carriers entered service in the immediate post-deregulation period.

[10]Using a cumulative Poisson probability distribution, significance tests were performed on accident rates contained in this, and subsequent, tables.

Table 2.2   Other Jet Carrier Service, Passenger Fatality and Aircraft Accident Rates, Domestic Scheduled Service

	Former Intrastate and Charters[a]		New Entrants
	1970-1978	1979-1985	1979-1985
Passenger Fatalities per 1 Million Enplanements	12.47	0.01[b,c]	1.12[d,e]
Passenger Serious Injuries per 1 Million Enplanements	0.00	0.05	0.05
Fatal Accidents per 1 Million Aircraft Departures	5.89	0.50[b]	1.49
Serious Injury Accidents per 1 Million Aircraft Departures	0.00	1.51	0.00
Minor Accidents per 1 Million Aircraft Departures	5.89	1.01[b]	2.24[c]

[a]Air California, Arrow, Capitol Air, Pacific Southwest, Southwest, and World.
[b]The 1979-1985 Former Intrastate and Charters rate is lower than the 1970-1978 rate at the 95 percent confidence level.
[c]The 1979-1985 Former Intrastate and Charters rate is lower than the 1979-1985 Trunk and Local Service rate (table 2.1) at the 95 percent confidence level.
[d]The 1979-1985 New Entrants rate is lower than the 1970-1978 Former Intrastate and Charters rate at the 95 percent confidence level.
[e]The 1979-1985 New Entrants rate is lower than the 1979-1985 Former Intrastate and Charters rate at the 90 percent confidence level.

Source: Derived from NTSB accident data; U.S. CAB, Forms 41 and 298; and Regional Airline Association, Annual Reports, various years.

Concern was voiced that these new entrants would adversely affect safety because of their inexperience in terms of pilot training, operations, and fleet maintenance. Table 2.2 suggests the new entrants did experience more passenger fatalities per 1 million passenger enplanements and more fatal accidents and minor accidents per 1 million aircraft departures than did either the trunk and local service carriers or the former intrastate and charter carriers. These rates, however, were not significantly higher. In addition, it should be noted that these rates are based on five total accidents, two of which involved fatalities, highlighting the relatively small number of enplanements and departures accounted for by the new entrants.

Even if the former intrastate and charter carriers and new entrant carriers were included with the trunk and local service carriers for the 1970-1985 period, there would be little impact on the five safety measures shown in Table 2.1 because of the small number of operations and accidents for these carriers. For example, in the 1970-1978 period there were only two accidents involving former intrastate and charter carriers. In the 1979-1985 period there were six accidents among the former intrastate and charter carriers and five among the new entrant carriers.

The conclusion that airline safety has improved does not seem particularly sensitive to the choice of measure; both passenger enplanement-based rates and aircraft departure-based rates declined between the pre- and post-deregulation periods. The declines in aggregate accident, fatality, and injury rates, however, do not unequivocally demonstrate that deregulation did not have an adverse impact on safety. Airline safety has been improving steadily since airline service began, reflecting advances in aircraft technology, navigational aids, weather detection equipment, and pilot training. It is possible that this steady decrease in aggregate safety rates offsets increases in certain types of accidents resulting from deregulation. To assess fully deregulation's effects on safety, the mechanisms by which deregulation might be expected to increase accidents in the wake of deregulation must be examined.

CAUSES OF AVIATION ACCIDENTS

Examining and comparing overall safety rates is useful for identifying segments of the industry where safety performance is worse than elsewhere and can be useful for assessing whether safety is improving or worsening over time. Overall rates, however, provide little understanding about why safety has been worse in some segments than in others, and they provide little guidance about where to focus efforts to improve safety. A more promising approach begins with classifying accidents according to their cause and comparing the distribution of causes both over time and across segments of the industry.

The most difficult problem in conducting such an analysis is how to assign a single cause for accidents, many of which have several contributing factors. There are three principal approaches to assigning cause; each has its drawbacks. Consider the example where an aircraft engine fails during takeoff and the pilot fails to take the proper action to land the plane safely. Obviously, both the engine failure and the pilot error caused the accident. Had there been no engine failure, there would have been no accident. Had the pilot acted properly, there would have been no accident.

The approach used in this analysis is to select the cause that initiated the sequence of events that culminated in the accident—in this case engine failure. An alternative approach would be to select as the cause the last point at which the accident could have been prevented—in this case the failure of the pilot to take the proper steps. Still another approach is to consider both as "the" cause.

How do these approaches differ? One clear difference from the example is that pilot error will show up as a cause much more often if either of the last two approaches is used, whereas equipment failure will show up more often if the first approach is used. Admittedly, there are many accidents initiated by equipment failure that a pilot should have been able to prevent through flying skills. However, the approach used in this analysis focuses on identifying the sequence-initiating cause. Focusing on the sequence-initiating cause avoids some data classification problems. Pilot error accidents identified under this methodology are due to "unforced" pilot error rather than "forced" pilot error. In the example, the fact the pilot failed to respond appropriately to an engine failure is considered a direct result of the pressure and stress associated with the emergency. Focusing on the cause as the last point at which the accident could have been prevented mixes both forced and unforced pilot errors. Counting all contributing causes for each accident makes interpretation of the distribution of causes difficult since some accidents have many contributing causes and, therefore contribute more causes to the distribution than others.

For each accident, the information from the NTSB accident investigation was examined and a sequence-initiating cause was determined.[11] Each accident was placed into one of the following nine categories:

- Equipment Failure
- Seatbelt Not Fastened
- Environment
- Pilot Error
- Air Traffic Control
- Ground Crew Error
- Other Aircraft
- Company Operations
- Other

[11]A detailed discussion of the procedures used is contained in Appendix B.

Equipment Failure

If the accident was precipitated by some sort of mechanical or electrical malfunction in the aircraft, then it was considered equipment failure. In some cases, such as improper installation of a part or failure to detect cracks or corrosion, more meticulous maintenance might have prevented the equipment failure. In other cases, such as failure of a tire that did not show excessive wear, maintenance practices could not reasonably be blamed. No attempt was made to distinguish whether inadequate maintenance was at fault.

Seatbelt Not Fastened

A surprisingly common source of serious passenger injury, but rarely death, is passengers not having their seatbelts fastened when turbulence is encountered. Such injuries include broken ankles, broken legs (in one case both legs), and head and neck injuries. If the seatbelt sign was illuminated in sufficient time for passengers to return to their seats and fasten their seatbelts, accidents were placed in this category. If the turbulence was unexpected and the seatbelt sign was not on, however, accidents were placed in the "environment" category.

Environment

Weather is a factor in many airline accidents but weather is frequently not regarded by the NTSB as the cause of the accident. Rather, the NTSB often determines the cause to be the cockpit crew not responding properly to weather conditions. The approach taken for this study differs from the NTSB approach in that accidents were rarely classified as "pilot error" if weather was a sequence-initiating factor. Thus an accident was usually classified as weather even if the pilot making precisely the right response at precisely the right time could have prevented the accident.

There were, however, some notable exceptions to this rule. If an aircraft took off under weather conditions that led to a takeoff accident—as were the cases with an Air Florida accident in January 1982 at Washington National Airport and a Commuter Airlines accident in March 1970 in Binghamton, New York—then the accident was considered pilot error. The argument for identifying pilot error as the sequence-initiating cause in these cases was that the pilot was safely on the ground and could have avoided the weather risk by delaying departure until the weather improved.

On the other hand, if an aircraft was unable to stop after landing on a slick runway, weather was considered the sequence-initiating cause, unless the pilot precipitated the accident by landing excessively long on the runway, as was the case with a Sunbird Airlines accident in Hickory, North Carolina, in May 1984. As a final example, if a pilot attempted to land when the airport was below minimum visibility and an alternate airport was available, pilot error was considered the sequence-initiating cause.[12]

Another form of environmental hazard is the threat of animal strikes. Animal strikes are rare among jet carriers and typically involve birds. Animal strikes are more common in general aviation (see Chapter 3) and are most likely to involve deer than birds. There have been some unusual cases, however, including an attack on a plane by a water buffalo in Southeast Asia and accidents in North America caused by striking a wide variety of animals including cattle, dogs, rabbits, buzzards, sea gulls, and geese.

Pilot Error

In addition to the weather-related examples cited earlier, pilot error was identified as the sequence-initiating cause only in those accidents where the error appeared undeniable. For example, pilot error is indicated for an accident caused by a pilot attempting a landing without lowering the landing gear or taxiing into a stationary object. Another example of pilot error involves running out of fuel because of failure to refuel or failure to switch fuel tanks during flight.

Air Traffic Control

Air traffic control was identified as the sequence-initiating cause when normal action by a controller could have prevented the accident. For example, a USAir accident in June 1976 in Philadelphia could have been avoided if air traffic control had not failed to advise the flight of unsafe weather.

Ground Crew

Accidents assigned to a ground crew sequence-initiating cause included such cases as the American Airlines accident at O'Hare

---

[12]The distinction between weather and pilot error is certainly the most difficult and subjective decision required in this analysis, but considerable effort was made to achieve consistency in the classifications over the study period and across industry segments.

in October 1978, where a service truck collided with a parked aircraft, and the Tampa Air accident in Tampa, Florida, in January 1972, where a ground crew member walked into a spinning propeller while delivering a message to the pilot of an aircraft about to depart.

Other Aircraft

Other aircraft are identified as the sequence-initiating cause in those accidents where the accident would not have occurred had another aircraft not been operating in the area. In the case of Part 121 and 135 operations, all accidents in this category involved general aviation aircraft. Examples include the PSA collision with a general aviation aircraft during approach into San Diego in 1978 or the 1981 Air U.S. collision with a general aviation aircraft carrying skydivers over Loveland, Colorado. This determination does not necessarily imply that the other aircraft was at fault, rather, that its presence initiated the accident.

Company Operations

A consistently incorrect operation or procedure on the part of the company owning or operating the aircraft or repeated improper actions by company personnel were classified as "company operations." Company operations were cited as the sequence-initiating cause only in a few cases such as when proper maintenance and inspection procedures were consistently lacking or when undue pressure for flight completion was routinely put on pilots and crew.

Other

Accidents not falling into one of the preceding categories were classified as "other." Such accidents included a wide array of causes ranging from a passenger tripping over a baby bottle in the aisle to injuries sustained during an evacuation due to a bomb threat.

TRUNK AND LOCAL SERVICE CARRIERS BEFORE AND AFTER DEREGULATION

Table 2.3 shows the combined accident rates for trunk and local service airlines broken down among the nine causes. The accident

Table 2.3   Jet Carrier Service, Total Accident Rate by Cause, Domestic Scheduled Service

| | Accidents per 1 Million Aircraft Departures | | |
| | Trunk and Local Service | | All Domestic Jet Service |
Cause	1970-1978	1979-1985	1986-1988
Equipment Failure	1.49	0.43	0.67
Seatbelt Not Fastened	1.49	0.68	0.50
Environment	0.82	0.33	0.62
Pilot Error	0.54	0.21	0.45
Air Traffic Control	0.26	0.11	0.11
Ground Crew Error	0.23	0.11	0.17
Other Aircraft	0.10	0.04	0.11
Company Operations	0.00	0.00	0.11
Other	0.39	0.50	0.17
Total	5.28	2.42[a]	2.91
Number of Accidents	205	66	52

[a]The 1979-1985 Trunk and Local Service rate is lower than the 1970-1978 rate at the 90 percent confidence level.

Source: Derived from NTSB accident data; U.S. CAB, Form 41.

rates for the trunk and local service carriers were lower for seven of the nine causes in the 1979-1985 period. Similarly, the accident rates for all domestic jet service during 1986-1988 were lower for seven of nine causes than trunk and local service rates in the 1970-1978 period. While none of the changes in accident rates by cause were statistically significant, the reduction in the aggregate 1979-1985 trunk and local service rate was.

Perhaps the most striking observation appears in the first line in the Table 2.3. The rate for equipment failure related accidents in the first six years following deregulation is less than one third of the pre-deregulation rate. The 1986-1988 rate is less than one half the pre-deregulation rate. If deregulation had indeed induced shortcuts in aircraft maintenance, the rate of equipment failures might be expected to have increased. The sharp decline in this rate suggests that, at least through 1988, deregulation has not led to widespread maintenance deficiencies.

Accident rates declined in the air traffic control category, reducing the already low rate even further. In terms of accidents, there is no evidence that the air traffic control system has functioned less safely after deregulation than it did before. This finding runs counter to claims that the PATCO strike, in August 1981, has degraded the safety performance of the nation's air traffic control system.[13] Similarly, the rate of accidents involving other aircraft, specifically general aviation aircraft, has not increased since deregulation. Thus despite the added pressure on the air traffic control system and on the airspace surrounding large airports because of hubbing-induced bunching of flights, the rates for the types of accidents that might be expected to have increased have, in fact, remained virtually the same.

Deregulation has also stimulated increased pressure on airline labor for less restrictive work rules. Pilots and cabin attendants are flying more hours per month and ground crews are performing a wider variety of tasks than they were prior to deregulation.[14] Despite these pressures, the rates for pilot error and ground crew error both declined in the 1979-1985 period. The rate for accidents where the seatbelt was not fastened has also declined, suggesting that, if anything, cabin attendants have been more effective in making sure that passengers fasten their seatbelts when turbulence is expected.

Although the changes in accident rates between the 1979-1985 period and the 1986-1988 period are small, some are suggestive of potential problems. For example, the rapid growth in air travel in the latter period caused some jet airlines to reach down into the commuter ranks for pilots more frequently than before. Some concern has been raised that less experienced and perhaps less qualified pilots were moving into the jet carrier ranks as a result. It is interesting, therefore, that the pilot error rate is twice as high in 1986-1988 as it was in 1979-1985. Similarly, as discussed in Chapter 7, concerns about aging aircraft increased markedly following the Aloha Airlines accident in April 1988. In light of this and of concerns about carrier finances (discussed in Chapter 6), it is also interesting to note that the rate of equipment failure accidents was 50 percent higher in 1986-1988 than it had been in 1979-1985.

[13]Admittedly part of the post-deregulation period was prior to the PATCO strike, but the expectation is that the accident rate for the entire 1979-1985 period would reflect any negative effects.

[14]Meyer and Oster, *Deregulation and the Future of Intercity Passenger Travel*, pp. 83-107.

COMMUTERS BEFORE AND AFTER DEREGULATION

The commuter industry is composed of about 200 carriers of greatly varying sizes, fleet mixes, and route structures.[15] The largest twenty commuters carry over half of all commuter passengers and the largest fifty carry over three quarters. As can be seen in Table 2.4, safety in the commuter industry improved significantly following deregulation. The principal reason for the improvement is almost certainly the tightening of commuter safety regulations in 1978. Table 2.4 also demonstrates that safety rates within the commuter industry have been inversely related to carrier size both before and after deregulation. In the 1970-1978 period, the top twenty carriers were more than four and a half times safer than the rest of the top fifty carriers (carriers twenty-one through fifty ranked by size) in terms of passenger fatalities per 1 million enplanements, and more than 19 times safer than the rest of the industry (the relatively small carriers who make up the non-top-fifty category). In terms of passenger serious injuries per 1 million enplanements, the top twenty carriers were almost two and a half times safer than the rest of the top fifty carriers and more than four and a half times safer than the rest of the industry.

Just as the commuter industry as a whole experienced an improvement in safety both in terms of fatalities and serious injuries after deregulation, each of these segments of the industry also experienced improvements. The safest portion of the industry in the pre-deregulation period, the top twenty commuters, experienced the smallest improvement in its safety record in the first six years following deregulation, most likely because these largest commuter carriers had previously instituted many of the procedures contained in the safety revisions mandated for Part 135 operators in 1978. Thus, these safety revisions had little additional effect on this group after 1978. On the other hand, the dramatic improvement in safety records for the rest of the top fifty and the rest of the industry in the first six years following deregulation are most likely the direct result of the 1978 safety revisions.

The FAA's commuter safety revisions in 1978 evolved from a review of safety regulations that was prompted in part by a 1972

---

[15]Unlike the jet carrier anlysis, which includes operations in all fifty states, the commuter carrier analysis focuses on operations in the contiguous forty-eight states. The distinction between commuter operations in the continental United States and those in Alaska and Hawaii is based on the belief that the flying environments faced in the latter are significantly different than the former. This is due to more adverse weather conditions, harsher terrain, and fewer airport navigation aids. Commuter operations in Alaska are examined in Chapter 4.

Table 2.4 Commuter Carriers, Passenger Fatality and Serious Injury Rates

	1970-1978	1979-1985	1986-1988
Total Industry:			
Passenger Fatalities per 1 Million Enplanements	2.65	1.27	0.38[a]
Passenger Serious Injuries per 1 Million Enplanements	1.62	0.66	0.28
Top Twenty Carriers:			
Passenger Fatalities per 1 Million Enplanements	0.69	0.67	0.12[a,b]
Passenger Serious Injuries per 1 Million Enplanements	0.93	0.21	0.17
Rest of the Top Fifty:			
Passenger Fatalities per 1 Million Enplanements	3.27	1.21	0.33[a]
Passenger Serious Injuries per 1 Million Enplanements	2.27	0.48[c]	0.51[d]
Rest of the Industry:			
Passenger Fatalities per 1 Million Enplanements	13.32	4.08[e]	4.67[a]
Passenger Serious Injuries per 1 Million Enplanements	4.30	3.00	0.55[a,b]

[a]The 1986-1988 rate is lower than the 1970-1978 rate at the 95 percent confidence level.
[b]The 1986-1988 rate is lower than the 1979-1985 rate at the 95 percent confidence level.
[c]The 1979-1985 rate is lower than the 1970-1978 rate at the 90 percent confidence level.
[d]The 1986-1988 rate is lower than the 1970-1978 rate at the 90 percent confidence level.
[e]The 1979-1985 rate is lower than the 1970-1978 rate at the 95 percent confidence level.

Source: Derived from NTSB accident data; U.S. CAB, Forms 41 and 298; and Regional Airline Association, Annual Reports, various years.

NTSB report.[16] The report pointed out inadequacies in FAA regulation of commuter airlines, including: (1) requirements for maintenance and training programs for crew members, (2) pilot qualification requirements, and (3) minimum equipment lists and

[16]National Transportation Safety Board, "Air Taxi Safety Study" (Washington, D.C: NTSB-AAS-72-6, 1972) and National Transportation Safety Board, "Special Study: Commuter Airline Safety, 1970-1979" (Washington, D.C.: NTSB-AAS-80-1, 1980).

flight continuation rules. Among the FAA's 1978 revisions was a provision requiring the pilot in command of a commuter aircraft seating ten or more passengers to hold an airline transport pilot (ATP) certificate rather than simply a commercial pilot certificate and a provision requiring a pilot in command to have made three takeoffs and three landings in the same type of aircraft within ninety days preceding a scheduled flight. Similarly, initial and recurrent training programs became a basic requirement in 1978. Commuter pilot requirements were brought more in line with those for jet airline pilots. Revised maintenance requirements included more detailed and extensive procedures for all types and classes of aircraft used by commuter operators as well as additional maintenance record keeping. Minimum equipment lists for commuters were also established for the first time in the 1978 FAA revisions.[17] These addressed such items as ground proximity warning systems and fire extinguishers, as well as radio and navigational equipment for IFR operations. Some additional regulatory changes included: more complete recordkeeping, including a log of mechanical irregularities, assignment of specific emergency duties for each crew member, and cockpit checklists. Larger commuter aircraft were equipped with cockpit voice recorders, onboard airborne thunderstorm detection equipment, and onboard weather radar.

As the final column of Table 2.4 indicates, the commuter industry improved substantially in the 1986-1988 period. The passenger fatality rate for the top twenty carriers fell to one fifth the 1979-1985 rate and was slightly better than the jet rate for the same period (Table 2.1). The rest of the top fifty carriers also improved in 1986-1988, with their passenger fatality rate less than 30 percent of their 1979-1985 rate. Only the smallest carriers in the industry failed to improve their fatality rate.

Table 2.5 breaks down the passenger fatality rate for the entire commuter industry into the nine cause categories for the 1970-1978 pre-deregulation period, the 1979-1985 immediate post-deregulation period, and the 1986-1988 period. As the table indicates, most of the improvement in the commuter airline passenger fatality rates between the pre-deregulation and immediate post-deregulation period came from a reduction in fatalities due to three reasons: equipment failure, pilot error, and weather. Given the thrust of many of the 1978 revisions, the pattern of fatality rate reductions in Table 2.5 might have been expected. The tightened maintenance procedures have probably contributed

---

[17]Minimum equipment lists are those items on the aircraft that must be functional for a flight to operate.

Table 2.5   Commuter Carriers, Passenger Fatality Rate by Cause,
Domestic Scheduled Service

Cause	Fatalities per 1 Million Enplanements		
	1970-1978	1979-1985	1986-1988
Equipment Failure	1.07	0.35	0.00
Seatbelt Not Fastened	0.00	0.00	0.00
Environment	0.61	0.27	0.00
Pilot Error	0.46	0.05	0.31
Air Traffic Control	0.04	0.00	0.00
Ground Crew Error	0.00	0.01	0.00
Other Aircraft	0.22	0.20	0.07
Company Operations	0.00	0.00	0.00
Other	0.24	0.39	0.00
Total	2.65	1.27	0.38[a]

[a]The 1986-1988 rate is lower than the 1970-1978 rate at the 95 percent confidence level.

Source: Derived from NTSB accident data; U.S. CAB, Forms 41 and 298; and Regional
Airline Association, Annual Reports, various years.

to the reduction in accidents involving equipment failure. The
added pilot certification requirements coupled with added recurrent
training have likely contributed to both reduced pilot error and
reduced weather-related fatalities. Weather-related fatalities may
have also been reduced by tightened regulations regarding onboard weather detection equipment and navigational equipment
for IFR flights.

The sources of improvement in commuter safety between the
1979-1985 and 1986-1988 periods can be seen in the final column
of Table 2.5. The accident rates for equipment failure, environment,
and other all fell to zero in the 1986-1988 period. While zero rates
cannot be expected to persist indefinitely, the improved equipment
failure and perhaps the environment rates may be due in part to
the spread of a new generation of reliable turboprops, many in the

thirty- to forty-seat size class, through the commuter fleet. On the other hand, the rate of pilot error increased in the 1986-1988 period. The same growth in travel demand, that pulled pilots from commuters to jet carriers at an accelerated rate, has caused commuters to reach down into the ranks of pilots in air taxis and cargo operators at a faster rate. In the same way an influx of less-experienced pilots from commuters may have increased pilot error in jet carriers, an influx of replacement commuter pilots from air taxis and cargo operators may have increased commuter pilot error rates.

Table 2.6 shows the 1979-1988 passenger fatality rate by type of accident for three segments of the commuter industry: the top twenty carriers, the rest of the top fifty and the rest of the commuter industry. The most striking pattern in the table is the markedly poorer safety record of the carriers outside of the top fifty. The pattern suggests that even with the tightened FAA regulations, the larger carriers may still have more effective operating and maintenance practices than the smallest carriers have been able to achieve.

One possible reason for the higher rate of equipment failure among the smallest carriers is that they are least likely to operate a fleet of all turbine-engine aircraft and more likely to operate small piston-engine aircraft seating nine or fewer passengers. Previous research has shown that small carriers operating either piston-engine aircraft only or a combined fleet of both piston- and turbine-engine aircraft experience a much higher rate of passenger fatalities than do either larger carriers operating any type of fleet or smaller carriers operating turbine-engine only fleets.[18] Piston engines have far more moving parts and are more complex to maintain. Moreover, a mixed fleet of both piston and turbine engines reduces the ability to develop specialized maintenance capabilities, while increasing spare parts inventory problems.

It is interesting that the smallest carriers also experience a substantially higher rate of fatalities from weather-related accidents. Again, it may be that the smaller piston-engine aircraft usually operated by these carriers are more difficult to operate in adverse weather than the larger aircraft usually flown by the largest carriers. In addition, these smaller aircraft may not be equipped with the same weather detection equipment and navigational equipment for instrument flights.

Many of the 1978 FAA revisions did not apply to aircraft seating nine or fewer passengers, so that their operators are not

---

[18]John R. Meyer and Clinton V. Oster, Jr., *Deregulation and the New Airline Entrepreneurs* (Cambridge: The MIT Press, 1984), pp. 97-99.

Table 2.6 Commuter Carriers, Passenger Fatality Rate by Cause, 1979-1988 Domestic Scheduled Service, Top Twenty versus Rest of Top Fifty versus Rest of Industry

	Fatalities per 1 Million Enplanements		
Cause	Top Twenty	Rest of Top Fifty	Rest of Industry
Equipment Failure	0.06[a]	0.30	0.93
Seatbelt Not Fastened	0.00	0.00	0.00
Environment	0.08[b]	0.02[c]	0.98
Pilot Error	0.05[b]	0.14	0.93
Air Traffic Control	0.00	0.00	0.00
Ground Crew Error	0.01	0.00	0.00
Other Aircraft	0.04[a]	0.26	0.52
Company Operations	0.00	0.00	0.00
Other	0.17	0.12	0.83
Total	0.41[b]	0.84	4.19

[a]The Top Twenty rate is lower than the Rest of Top Fifty and Rest of Industry rates at the 95 percent confidence level.
[b]The Top Twenty rate is lower than the Rest of Industry rate at the 95 percent confidence level.
[c]The Rest of the Top Fifty rate is lower than the Rest of Industry rate at the 95 percent confidence level.

Source: Derived from NTSB accident data; U.S. CAB, Forms 41 and 298; and Regional Airline Association, Annual Reports, various years.

subject to some of the same tighter maintenance requirements.[19] Indeed, even aircraft seating ten to nineteen passengers had somewhat less extensive requirements than did larger aircraft, a difference that may have contributed to some accidents.[20] Recent trends toward affiliation of commuter carriers with major airlines

[19]U.S. General Accounting Office, "Safety Standards on Small Passenger Aircraft—With Nine or Fewer Seats—Are Significantly Less Stringent than on Larger Aircraft" (Washington, D.C.: GAO/RCED-84-2, 1984).
[20]National Transportation Safety Board, "Safety Recommendation A-86-98 through A-86-118" (Washington, D.C., 1986) and "NTSB Recommends Improvements in Commuter Safety Standards," *Aviation Week and Space Technology*, October 6, 1986, pp. 31, 32.

may serve to enhance the maintenance requirements of the smaller commuter operators to the degree that the major airline maintenance and safety programs are extended to the commuter affiliate.

Given the apparent increase in commuter safety after extension of regulations in 1978 to the larger carriers and the poor relative safety record of the smallest carriers, further improvements in safety might be achieved by extending coverage of such regulations to smaller carriers and particularly smaller aircraft types. Given the substantially higher probabilities of equipment failure in the smallest commuter aircraft, such requirements might be expected to have significant safety benefits, although they might also increase the cost of service to small communities.

COMMUTER SUBSTITUTION AND SAFETY

If commuters were a homogeneous segment of the air transportation industry, there would be little to refute the claim of serious degradation of safety as commuter airlines replaced jet carriers in small communities. However, the commuter industry has clear and systematic differences in safety performance among its various segments. Relying solely on the aggregate commuter safety record may be misleading and suggest that safety degradation is worse than it truly is. Since the larger commuter carriers have safety rates approaching those of jet carriers, the impact on safety would be less adverse if replacement service is provided by this segment of the commuter industry.

Table 2.7 summarizes the experience between 1978 and 1986 in sixty city-pair markets involving fifty communities that lost jet carrier service between June 1978 and June 1984 and where commuter carriers provided replacement service in 1986. Most of the replacement service involved the largest commuter carriers, mainly because they had the personnel, equipment, and expertise to move most easily into markets abandoned by the jet carriers. In fifty-four of the sixty markets, replacement service was provided by either a carrier affiliated with a jet carrier through a code-sharing relationship or an independent top twenty commuter.[21]

An important consideration overlooked thus far in the discussion of safety implications of commuter replacement stems from the improved service typically offered to small communities by commuters. As Table 2.7 indicates, commuter replacement

---

[21]For a further discussion of these code-sharing alliances see Clinton V. Oster, Jr. and Don N. Pickrell, "The Effects of Code Sharing on Competition in the Regional Airline Industry," *Transporation Research*, 22A (6) (November 1988): 405-417.

Table 2.7 Transition from Jet Service to Commuter Service, Sixty City-Pair Markets Where Commuters Replaced Jets

	1978	1986
Average Weekday Departures	2.88	6.29
Average Intermediate Stops	0.59	0.30

Source: U.S. CAB Staff Study. "Report on Airline Service, Fares, Traffic, Load Factors and Market Shares, Service Status on September 1, 1984" (Washington, D.C.: U.S. Government Printing Office, December 1984); and Official Airline Guide, North American Edition, July 1, 1978 and 1986 editions.

service into these communities resulted in an increase in frequency of weekday flights to these cities, improving this aspect of air transportation services. In addition, the average number of intermediate stops on flights between the small community and its nearest major hub decreased by almost half after the transition to commuter service. Thus on average, service has improved in these communities where commuters provided substitute service for jets because passengers have more direct connections to hubs where they can link up with jet carrier service.

The data in Table 2.7 not only indicate improved service when commuters substitute for jets in small communities, but the data also suggest that a straight comparison between jet carrier and commuter safety measures is not appropriate. If the service improvement includes fewer intermediate stops on flights to and from these small communities on commuter flights, the relative safety rates of commuters and jet carriers must be adjusted to reflect the additional risk from extra takeoffs and landings on the jet flights. According to Table 2.7 the average number of takeoffs and landings associated with jet service to these small communities was 1.59 (the original takeoff and subsequent landing and an average of 0.59 takeoffs and landings at intermediate stops), but only 1.30 for commuters serving the same cities. Thus, to take account of the added risk from more takeoffs and landings during the jet trip, the jet carrier rate should be inflated by 22 percent. So, while there may be some increased risk associated with the service provided by commuters relative to that provided by jet carriers, there is not the dramatic effect suggested by a simple comparison of aggregate safety measures.

A final consideration must be added to complete this safety comparison. As a result of the increased frequency of service offered in small communities in the wake of the exit of jet carriers, ridership was generally found to increase. The added convenience offered by commuters' more frequent and better timed service attracted passengers who had previously opted for the automobile. It seems reasonable to assume that the average commuter flight length of between 120 and 130 miles substitutes for an auto trip to the same hub airport of about 150 miles. Further assuming that average auto occupancy for such a trip is about 1.5 (slightly below the average for all intercity auto trips), the fatality rate associated with motor vehicle trips that would be appropriate to compare to the commuter rate is somewhere between 1.9 and 2.3 passenger fatalities per 1 million passenger trips. Comparing this motor vehicle fatality rate to that of the top-fifty-commuter fatality rate indicates that travel is safer for those passengers switching from autos to commuter airlines as a result of improved air service. Thus, in some cases, commuter service to small communities may actually improve the transportation safety record relative to the prior service by jet aircraft. Indeed, if following replacement by a top twenty commuter carrier, 20 percent of the commuter's passengers were drawn from auto travel and the rest from jet travel, the net effect would be improved rather than degraded safety.

While the safety of scheduled airline service commands most of the public attention, the jet airline and commuter segments of the industry are the safest segments and produce only about 12 percent of aviation industry fatalities. There are far more accidents and fatalities in the general aviation and charter segments of the aviation industry, and it is these segments that provide the training ground for scheduled airline pilots. The safety of charter service and general aviation is the topic of the next chapter.

Chapter 3

Charter Service and General Aviation

Most public attention to aviation safety has focused on scheduled passenger service provided by major airlines and commuter service. Little attention has been paid to other segments of the aviation industry. In the United States, however, only about 21 percent of aviation activity and 12 percent of aviation fatalities occur in the major airline and commuter segments of the industry. As can be seen in Figure 3.1, scheduled commuter airlines accounted for 3.5 percent of aircraft flight hours over the 1978-1989 period, nonscheduled air taxis logged 6.8 percent of flight hours, and scheduled jet airlines accounted for 17.6 percent of flight hours. General aviation was clearly the dominant segment of the industry, accounting for just over 71 percent of flight activity. General aviation also dominated the industry in terms of fatalities (Figure 3.2), accounting for nearly 79 percent of the 16,349 fatalities from aviation accidents during the 1978-1989 period, while scheduled jet airlines accounted for only about 10 percent.

Nonscheduled segments have amassed a consistently poorer safety record than have the scheduled portions of the aviation industry. As demonstrated in Figure 3.3, which shows the accident rates per 100,000 flight hours for each of the five industry segments over the 1978 through 1989 period, jet charter operations have a generally poorer safety record than do scheduled jet airline operations. Similarly, nonscheduled air taxi operations as a group have been consistently less safe than scheduled commuter airline operations throughout the period. Finally, general aviation

Figure 3.1 Aircraft Flight Hours by Industry Segment, 1978-1989

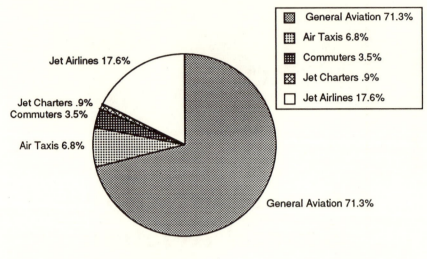

Jet Airlines 17.6%

Jet Charters .9%
Commuters 3.5%

Air Taxis 6.8%

General Aviation 71.3%

General Aviation 71.3%
Air Taxis 6.8%
Commuters 3.5%
Jet Charters .9%
Jet Airlines 17.6%

Source: 1988-89 NTSB Annual Reports

Figure 3.2 Aircraft Fatalities by Industry Segment, 1978-1989

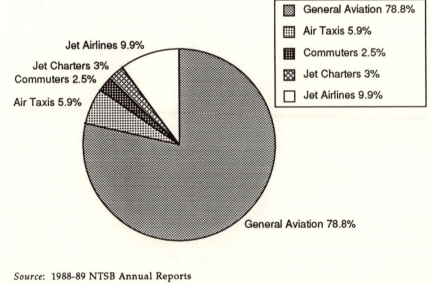

Jet Airlines 9.9%

Jet Charters 3%
Commuters 2.5%

Air Taxis 5.9%

General Aviation 78.8%

General Aviation 78.8%
Air Taxis 5.9%
Commuters 2.5%
Jet Charters 3%
Jet Airlines 9.9%

Source: 1988-89 NTSB Annual Reports

42

Figure 3.3 Accident Rates by Industry Segment, 1978-1989

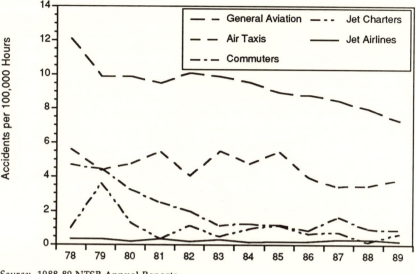

Source: 1988-89 NTSB Annual Reports

has had by far the worst safety record of any of these segments.[1]

A discussion of aviation safety would be clearly incomplete without carefully considering the nonscheduled segments of the industry. Not only do these segments account for most aviation fatalities and have the highest accident rates, but they also provide the training ground for most commuter and jet carrier pilots. This chapter examines the safety performance of three nonscheduled segments of the aviation industry: charter jet service, air taxis, and general aviation.

CHARTER JET SERVICE

Airline deregulation removed most economic regulation for scheduled operations with a resulting secondary effect on charter passenger operations. Prior to deregulation, major scheduled airlines were frustrated by the difficulty of obtaining new route authority from the CAB; as a result, airlines used nonscheduled

[1]Figure 3.3 is based on flight hours rather than takeoffs and landings. Because general aviation has much shorter flights, on average, than the other segments, its share of departures is even greater than its share of flight hours shown in Figure 3.1. Thus, general aviation's fatality rate based on departures would almost certainly be closer to the other segments, although it would still be worse.

charter operations to improve their equipment utilization in counterseasonal markets and to create new, albeit seasonal, business. With the advent of deregulation, scheduled carriers could enter new markets and serve counterseasonal routes on a scheduled basis, reducing their incentive to offer charter flights. In addition, deregulation's fare freedoms, and in particular the ability to offer discount fares on a controlled number of seats on each flight, gave price-sensitive vacation travelers a low-cost scheduled alternative to charter flights. Thus, in the post-deregulation period most scheduled airlines reduced their charter offerings, leaving the field largely to all charter carriers.

The charter jet portion of the industry includes both passenger and cargo operations in both domestic and international service. While the market potential for nonscheduled domestic passenger service may have become less attractive after deregulation, international nonscheduled service was less affected. By contrast, the nonscheduled domestic and international cargo markets, and particularly the overnight package express portions of those markets, have enjoyed strong growth in the past decade, in part due to air cargo deregulation that began in 1977.[2]

Because of differences in operating environments, the various segments of the nonscheduled jet carriers may well have different levels of safety performance than scheduled carriers. Unfortunately, accident and fatality rates for these segments cannot be compared because reliable operations data are not available for either domestic or international nonscheduled operations. The FAA collects operations data with a voluntary survey of nonscheduled operators, but the response rate is only approximately 60 percent. These nonscheduled operations data almost certainly contain systematic biases across industry segments, but there is no way to determine the direction or magnitude of these biases.

It is possible, however, to examine and compare the distribution of causes of nonscheduled jet accidents using the same approach to accident classification used in Chapter 2. Table 3.1 shows the share of accidents by each major cause category for Part 121 domestic and international charter and cargo operations. Part 121 cargo operations include service provided in large turboprop aircraft, but still meeting Part 121 operating regulations. For comparison, the shares of accidents by cause for domestic and international scheduled Part 121 service are also shown in the table.

[2]Clinton V. Oster, Jr. and Robin Miles-McLean, "Air Cargo: The Impacts of Adapting to Deregulation," *Transportation Research Record*, 1147 (1988).

Table 3.1 Distribution of Accident Cause by Part 121 Industry
Segment, 1970-1988

Cause	Percentage of Accidents[a]					
	Domestic Charter (%)	Intern'l Charter (%)	Domestic Cargo (%)	Intern'l Cargo (%)	Domestic Sched. (%)	Intern'l Sched. (%)
Equipment	45	55	30	42	24	20
Seatbelt	18	18	0	0	26	25
Environment	9	0	7	0	17	13
Pilot Error	18	0	46	21	12	21
Air Traffic Control	0	0	5	0	4	0
Ground Crew	0	0	7	11	5	4
Other Aircraft	0	9	2	5	4	4
Company Operations	0	0	2	5	1	2
Other	9	18	2	16	6	12
Number of Accidents	11	11	57	19	343	85

[a]Totals may not add to 100 percent due to rounding.

Source: Derived from NTSB Accident Data

The most striking feature of Table 3.1 is that equipment
failure is the largest causal factor and that the role of equipment
failure is larger for charter passenger operators than it is for
either scheduled airlines or cargo carriers. Weather and pilot
error are also important causes of charter accidents, particularly
on domestic flights, while failure to wear a seat belt is more likely
to cause injuries on long international flights. While these other
causes should not be ignored, the clear implication from the table
is that efforts to improve charter safety should focus heavily on
equipment inspection and maintenance.

By contrast, among Part 121 cargo operators, pilot error is a
far more important accident cause than it is for either charter or
scheduled carriers. The relatively high incidence of pilot error in

domestic cargo may be explained in part by the common practice of air cargo flights operating at night, thereby presenting pilots with a more difficult flight environment.

NONSCHEDULED COMMUTER SERVICE

Table 3.2 shows the distribution of accident causes for Part 135 charter operations (air taxis), Part 135 cargo operations, and scheduled commuters. Only domestic service in the forty-eight-state region is included in the table, as there is not enough international service to allow meaningful comparisons. Service in Alaska is discussed in the next chapter.

Table 3.2 Distribution of Accident Cause by Part 135 Industry Segment, 1983-1988

	Percent of Accidents[a]		
Cause	48-State Air Taxis (%)	48-State Cargo (%)	48-State Scheduled[b] (%)
Equipment	30	29	30
Seatbelt	0	0	c
Environment	11	8	14
Pilot Error	42	43	36
Air Traffic Control	1	0	c
Ground Crew	2	2	10
Other Aircraft	5	5	4
Company Operations	0	1	1
Other	9	12	2
Number of Accidents	139	173	140

[a]Totals may not add to 100 percent due to rounding.
[b]48-State Scheduled numbers are for 1979-1988.
[c]Less than 1 percent.

Source: Derived from NTSB Accident Data

For air taxi operators, pilot error, equipment failure, and environment are the major accident causes. In comparing air taxis with scheduled commuters, the most apparent difference is the larger role pilot error plays in air taxi accidents. The larger role for pilot error may be due to the requirement that scheduled commuter pilots have ATP ratings, where a commercial rating is sufficient for air taxi service. ATP-rated pilots typically have more experience and must pass stricter licensing standards. It is not an unusual career progression for less-experienced pilots to begin in air taxi service and move up to a scheduled commuter after accumulating experience. Recall from Chapter 2 that in 1987 and 1988, as pilots began moving from air taxis to commuters at a faster rate, the role of pilot error increased in the commuter ranks.

GENERAL AVIATION

In 1986, general aviation accounted for 97.8 percent of the U.S. civil aircraft fleet, with single-engine piston aircraft alone accounting for 78.1 percent of the fleet. General aviation accounted for 84.1 percent of aircraft departures, 71.5 percent of aircraft hours flown, and 50.7 percent of aircraft miles flown. Private and student pilots account for about 65 percent of the estimated 700,000 active pilots in the United States. About 36 percent of active pilots are instrument rated. In addition, many of the pilots holding commercial and air transport license ratings are also general aviation pilots.[3]

The widely held perception of general aviation being synonymous with recreational flying is not entirely accurate. Of the approximately 31 million hours of general aviation flying in 1985 in fixed-wing aircraft, only about 31 percent was "personal" flying. Executive and business flying accounted for another 39 percent, instructional flying for 16 percent, and aerial applications and observation for 11 percent, with the remaining 3 percent in other uses.[4]

Although, as seen in Figure 3.3, the general aviation accident rate appears to have declined slightly during the past decade, the combination of the number of people killed each year and the relatively high accident rate compared with other segments of aviation means that general aviation safety remains a serious

[3]Aircraft Owners and Pilots Association, *AOPA 1988 Aviation Fact Card* (Frederick, MD: Aircraft Owners and Pilots Association, 1988).
[4]Federal Aviation Administration, *FAA Statistical Handbook of Aviation* (Washington: Government Printing Office, 1985).

problem. The improvements in safety during the past decade in the scheduled portion of the aviation industry, which was already noted for its high levels of safety, offer hope that with similar attention and effort general aviation safety might also experience significant improvements.

General aviation accidents are analyzed using the same approach and classification scheme as for the other segments of U.S. aviation (Appendix B). For general aviation, only accidents during flights operating under general aviation regulations (14 CFR 91) in the contiguous forty-eight states plus Hawaii are included— Alaskan operations are examined separately and discussed later in this chapter. The general aviation accidents that are examined are further limited to airplanes, thereby excluding helicopters, gliders, ultralights, balloons, and gyrocopters. Two of the types of accidents—equipment failure, and pilot error—occur in sufficient number and are of sufficient concern that they are disaggregated into subcategories.

CAUSES OF GENERAL AVIATION ACCIDENTS

Table 3.3 compares the distribution of accidents by cause for general aviation with those for domestic scheduled jet service and domestic scheduled commuter service. As is the case with other segments of aviation, no classification scheme can account for the entire array of circumstances leading to injury or equipment damage in general aviation. Accidents not falling into one of the eight major categories are classified as "other" and include such causes as medical impairment from heart attacks, aircraft accidents during illegal drug transport, accidents by unlicensed pilots, and accidents where the cause was ambiguous or the aircraft was not recovered. For example, on June 9, 1985, in Melstone, Montana, a Piper PA-32R was observed in a left turn and a steep dive until it passed out of view and crashed behind a hill. The investigation revealed no evidence of airframe or engine malfunction prior to the crash but a medical exam revealed the pilot had 90 percent narrowing of both coronary arteries and evidence of hemorrhage. On February 3, 1985, a Piper PA-23 crashed into the Atlantic Ocean near Key Largo, Florida, and sank in fifteen feet of water. The pilot and passenger were pinned in the cabin by twenty-five bales of marijuana that shifted forward on impact.

The most striking feature in Table 3.3 is the role of pilot error. Pilot error accounted for 65 percent of general aviation accidents, but it accounted for only 11 percent of jet carrier accidents and 36

Table 3.3   Distribution of Accidents by Cause for Selected Industry Segments, 1979-1988[a]

	General Aviation[b] (%)	Domestic Scheduled Jets (%)	48-State Scheduled Commuter (%)
Equipment Failure	19	20	30
Seatbelt	0	24	c
Environment	7	19	14
Pilot Error	65	11	36
Air Traffic Control	c	6	c
Ground Crew	c	7	10
Other Aircraft	3	2	4
Company Operations	c	2	1
Other	6	9	2
Number of Accidents	12,407	127	140

[a]Totals may not add to 100 percent due to rounding.
[b]General Aviation accidents are from the 1983-1988 period.
[c]Less than 1 percent.

Source: Derived from NTSB Accident Data

percent of commuter accidents. While the greater role of pilot error in general aviation accidents might be expected, the magnitude of the difference is startling. Roughly two thirds of general aviation accidents are attributed to "unforced" errors by the pilot.

Several differences between general aviation pilots and jet carrier and commuter pilots may help explain the difference. All jet and commuter pilots have at least commercial license ratings and the vast majority have ATP ratings, whereas most general aviation pilots have either private or student licenses. Thus, the level of training and experience differs significantly. Moreover, jet pilots and, to a lesser extent, commuter pilots are trained extensively in emergency procedures in sophisticated simulators.

Such simulators allow training for a much broader range of situations than in-flight training to which general aviation pilots are limited. Finally, all jet operations and almost all of the commuter operations reflected in the table are in dual-piloted aircraft. While the presence of a second pilot presents potential crew coordination problems, a co-pilot is nevertheless an important asset in the safety of a flight.

A second difference evident in the table is the smaller role for environmental causes in general aviation. Moreover, the role of weather is even smaller than the table suggests. Virtually all of the environment accidents for jet carriers and commuters are weather accidents, whereas about half the general aviation environment accidents are collisions with animals (mostly deer) on the runway or are due to wind gusts overturning the aircraft during taxi.

At first, the greater role of weather in jet and commuter accidents appears surprising since these aircraft typically have greater capabilities to operate in adverse weather and the pilots have more training and experience in instrument flight conditions. However, general aviation flying does not have the same schedule pressures as the other segments represented in the table and a great many flights take place only if weather conditions pose no risks. Many general aviation pilots are likely to cancel or postpone their flights if weather is bad since the majority of general aviation pilots are not instrument rated. Also, many weather-related accidents are initiated by some other factor and therefore not categorized as environment in the analysis. For example, if a VFR-rated pilot initiates flight in marginal weather conditions, the resulting accident is classified as preflight judgment pilot error. If a VFR-rated pilot continues a flight into IFR conditions, the resulting accident is considered in-flight judgment pilot error. These, and other, subcategories of pilot error are discussed in the following section.

General Aviation Pilot Error

Pilot error includes a wide variety of situations. These accidents are divided into seven categories: flying skills, in-flight judgment, preflight judgment, fuel management, student pilot, homebuilt, and alcohol/drug.

Flying skills refer to deficiencies in maintaining physical control of the aircraft including hard landings, landing long on the runway, stalls, or taxiing into stationary objects. For example, on February 14, 1985, a Piper PA-23 departed Everglades City,

Florida, airport. Shortly after takeoff, the aircraft started a shallow turn to the left in a nose-high attitude, lost speed, and began rolling rapidly to the left. Post-impact investigation revealed no mechanical malfunctions. The pilot and two passengers were killed.

In-flight judgment refers to errors in judgment that put the aircraft into unnecessarily hazardous situations such as flying at extremely low altitudes, "buzzing" people on the ground, hitting power lines, choosing to land on uncertain terrain such as roads and pastures except in emergency situations, continuing a VFR flight into IFR conditions, and attempting to land at an airport that is below weather minimums when an alternate airport is available. For example, on July 12, 1985, in Columbus, Montana, a Piper J3C-65 was making a low pass over the passenger's home and the pilot pulled the aircraft up abruptly stalling the aircraft. The altitude was too low to allow recovery from the stall and both pilot and passenger were killed.

In-flight judgment also refers to failure to follow established procedures in flight such as not doing a landing checklist, failure to correct for carb icing, becoming lost in flight, and failure to maintain proper fuel mixture control. For example, on June 28, 1986, a pilot practicing single engine procedures in a Piper PA-23-160 forgot to lower the landing gear, recognized the error late in the approach, and landed with gear only partially extended.

Preflight judgment refers to errors in procedures or judgment that occur prior to the flight. These errors include failure to do a preflight checklist, failure to get a weather briefing, takeoff from rough terrain or the wrong runway, failure to check for water in the fuel, a noninstrument rated pilot taking off in poor weather conditions, and failure to brief passengers on procedures. For example, on March 14, 1985, in Logan, Utah, a noninstrument-rated pilot and two passengers departed under "extreme instrument meteorological conditions" with visibility reported as a few feet in ice fog. The plane, a Piper PA-28, crashed just after takeoff and all aboard were killed. Other examples include an August 7, 1986, accident involving a Piper PA-28-140 that crashed while attempting to takeoff from Phoenix, Arizona, while overloaded in high-density altitude conditions. On July 16, 1986, the pilot of a Beech 35, departing from Plymouth, Florida, failed to use a preflight checklist. The aircraft pulled up (rotated) early due to improper setting of elevator trim tab with a resulting stall and crash.

Fuel management includes all instances of running out of fuel in flight except for mechanical failures such as leaks or defective fuel cells. Misreading fuel gauges or inaccurate fuel gauges are considered fuel management, since fuel gauges on many general aviation aircraft are known not to be reliable in all flight conditions. For example, on April 15, 1985, in Worthington, Indiana, a Piper PA-30 stalled and crashed in a field after declaring an emergency from a power loss in the right engine. Postcrash investigation revealed the right engine fuel selector was positioned on the right main tank which was empty.

The student pilot category includes any accident due to pilot error by beginning student pilots. This classification includes pilots flying with an instructor or making one of their first four solo flights. For example, on April 2, 1985, a student pilot and a flight instructor were flying a Cessna 150L on a local instructional flight in Corona, California. The student had flown only a total of three hours prior to this flight. The aircraft was observed spinning toward the ground in a near vertical descent. Both pilot and student were killed. Postcrash investigation indicated no preimpact part failure or malfunction.

Homebuilt includes any pilot error accident in a homebuilt aircraft. For example, on February 1, 1986, a homebuilt airplane crashed in Owasso, Oklahoma. The pilot was reportedly checking the aircraft's stability for the owner by practicing Lazy 8 maneuvers when he lost control of the plane.

Finally, alcohol/drugs includes any accident when the pilot is impaired by alcohol or drugs. On June 25, 1985, in Reedsburg, Wisconsin, a Piper PA-28-151 crashed killing both pilot and passenger. Postcrash investigation found the pilot's blood alcohol level to be 0.239 percent.

Some insight into why pilot error is a much greater cause of accidents in general aviation than other segments can be gained by exploring the types of pilot error leading to general aviation accidents. The bottom line of Table 3.4 shows the share of total pilot error for both fatal and nonfatal accidents. As the table indicates, pilot error accounts for about the same percentage of both fatal (64) and nonfatal (65) accidents.

In part, the comparison of the contribution of pilot error accidents in different segments of aviation shown earlier in Table 3.3 might be misleading because the general aviation figure includes accidents by student pilots and accidents in homebuilt aircraft—types of accidents that are not found in commercial service. Similarly, the general aviation figure includes accidents where the pilot was under the influence of alcohol or drugs. While such accidents are possible in commercial service, they are extremely rare. As can be seen in Table 3.4, however, even if accidents from these three causes are removed, pilot error is still a much greater

Table 3.4 General Aviation Pilot Error Accidents by Type of Pilot Error, 1983-1988

Type of Pilot Error	Number of Fatal Pilot Error Accidents	Percentage of Total General Aviation Fatal Accidents (%)	Number of Nonfatal Pilot Error Accidents	Percentage of Total General Aviation Nonfatal Accidents (%)
Flying Skills	256	11	2279	23
In-Flight Judgment	445	18	1026	10
Preflight Judgment	498	20	967	10
Fuel Management	66	3	867	9
Alcohol/Drugs	140	6	54	1
Student Pilot	90	4	1144	11
Homebuilt	58	2	127	1
Total Pilot Error	1,553	64	6,464	65

Source: Derived from NTSB Accident Data

factor in general aviation than it is in commercial service. Taken together, these three types of accidents account for only 12 percent of fatal accidents and 13 percent of nonfatal accidents. Alcohol or drug use may account for a somewhat higher share of accidents, particularly nonfatal accidents, than is indicated in the table since pilots are not routinely tested for alcohol or drugs after accidents.

Looking at the remaining causes in Table 3.4 reveals that deficiencies in flying skills are the major cause of nonfatal accidents but only the third leading cause of fatal accidents. A great many flying skills accidents occur in the landing phase when a pilot lands too far down the runway and runs off the end, lands short of the runway, flares too soon and makes a hard landing, or fails to maintain directional control during either the landing roll or the takeoff roll. Such accidents frequently do substantial damage to the aircraft and may produce injuries, but only about 11 percent of fatal accidents are due to deficient flying skills. Those flying skills accidents that result in fatalities are more likely to occur during the takeoff and initial climb phases of flight and frequently involve stalling the aircraft or losing control during a turn at relatively low altitude.

Far more serious, in terms of fatalities, are errors in preflight judgment or in-flight judgment. In-flight judgment accidents account for 18 percent of fatal accidents. Nearly one third (30 percent) of all in-flight judgment accidents involve fatalities. A great many in-flight judgment accidents are associated with flying at very low altitude, often to buzz people on the ground. Perhaps greater sanctions against pilots who perform such maneuvers are warranted.

Preflight judgment accidents account for 20 percent of fatal accidents. Again, about one third (34 percent) of this type of accident result in fatalities. Most preflight judgment accidents are of two general types: failure to do a careful preflight check list or poor preflight judgment with respect to weather conditions. The prevalence and seriousness of these types of accidents suggest that more emphasis should be given to preflight check lists during pilot training. It also suggests that proposals to charge pilots for weather briefings or close some Flight Service Stations may result in more general aviation fatalities. Many accidents are caused by pilots failing to get a weather briefing and encountering unexpected bad weather. Making weather briefings more difficult or more expensive cannot help but increase this type of accident.

Finally, fuel management accidents are fairly common and usually result in substantial damage to the aircraft, but do not often result in fatalities. Most loss of power from fuel exhaustion occurs in level flight at altitudes sufficient to allow the pilot to select proper terrain for an emergency landing.

General Aviation Equipment Failure

As with other segments of aviation, if the events leading to a general aviation accident were initiated by some sort of mechanical, structural, or electrical malfunction in the aircraft, the accident is considered caused by equipment failure. Equipment failure accidents were further broken down into engine, instruments and electrical equipment, landing gear and tires, structure, homebuilt, and other categories.

Engine failure includes failure of the power plant including propellers, internal engine parts, carburetors, turbochargers, magnetos, exhaust systems, and fuel lines downstream of the fuel tank. For example, on July 6, 1986, a Piper PA-28-180 crashed five minutes after takeoff from York, Pennsylvania. The cause of the accident was determined to be engine seizure due to lack of engine oil as the result of in-flight disconnection of the sump quick drain. Instruments and electrical equipment includes any malfunction of aircraft instruments or any other electrical failure. For example, on May 4, 1986, a North American SNJ-5 crashed while en route to Oklahoma City, Oklahoma. The pilot radioed that he had smoke in the cockpit and was killed during an emergency landing in a field. Postcrash investigation revealed that the smoke was caused by an electrical short.

Landing gear and tires includes any malfunction of landing gear, tires, or brakes other than failure due to hard landings or excessive loads due to abrupt maneuvers. For example, on April 26, 1986, a Bellanca 14-19-3A landed in Lower Lake, California, with only the left landing gear extended although the gear indicator lights indicated all gear fully extended. Structure includes failure of wings, flight control surfaces, or other structural parts of the plane. For example, on March 21, 1985, a Beech B-35D over Mojave, California, experienced a separation of the left stabilizer assembly from the aircraft. The plane crashed killing the pilot and two passengers.

Homebuilt includes any mechanical, structural, or electrical failure of a homebuilt aircraft. For example, on June 24, 1985, in Cambridge, Minnesota, a pilot in an aircraft he designed and built experienced in-flight separation of both horizontal stabilizers and both wings with a resulting fatal crash.

Table 3.3 indicated that equipment failure accounted for 19 percent of general aviation accidents compared with a 20 percent share of accidents for domestic jet carriers and 30 percent share of accidents for commuter carriers. It is important to realize, however, that because the rate of general aviation accidents is so much higher, the rate of equipment failure per 100,000 flight hours is still higher for general aviation than it is for the other two segments even though the share is about the same or lower.

Table 3.5 explores equipment failure as a cause of general aviation accidents by reporting subcategories of equipment failure and examining equipment failure's contribution to both fatal and nonfatal accidents. While equipment failure accidents account for about one fifth of nonfatal accidents, they account for only 12 percent of fatal accidents. The major form of equipment failure is engine failure. The overwhelming majority of general aviation aircraft use piston engines. In commuter service, piston-powered aircraft have been found to be involved in proportionately more accidents than turbine-powered aircraft.[5] Piston engines are in many ways more complex and have more moving parts than do

[5]Clinton V. Oster, Jr. and C. Kurt Zorn, "Deregulation and Commuter Airline Safety," *Journal of Air Law and Commerce* 49 (2) (1983): 315-335.

Table 3.5 General Aviation Equipment Failure Accidents by Type of Equipment Failure, 1983-1988

Type of Equipment Failure	Number of Fatal Equipment Failure Accidents	Percentage of Total General Aviation Fatal Accidents (%)	Number of Nonfatal Equipment Failure Accidents	Percentage of Total General Aviation Nonfatal Accidents (%)
Engine	163	7	1,280	13
Instruments	26	1	90	1
Landing Gear	1	0	411	4
Structure	54	2	65	1
Homebuilt	40	2	149	1
Other	9	0	65	1
Total Equipment Failures	293	12	2,060	21

Source: Derived from NTSB Accident Data

the turboprop or jet engines. In addition to using piston engines, most general aviation aircraft have only a single engine whereas even the smallest aircraft used in scheduled commuter service is multiengined. Even so, only 11 percent of engine failure accidents result in fatalities. Far more serious, in terms of the proportion of accidents resulting in fatalities, are instrument and electrical failures, with structure failures by far the most serious.

GENERAL AVIATION IN ALASKA

Table 3.6 shows both the rates of fatal and nonfatal accidents and the distribution of causes for Alaskan general aviation operations and for operations in the continental U.S. Looking first at the last line of the table, the fatal accident rate in Alaska is only slightly higher than that outside of Alaska, but the nonfatal accident rate is twice as high. Pilot error is the major cause throughout and the shares are not dramatically different in Alaska than elsewhere. Equipment failures are less common in Alaska, but, not surprisingly, environment is a more frequent cause. The larger proportion of fatal accidents in the "Other" category in Alaska reflects a larger

Table 3.6 General Aviation in Alaska, Distribution of Accidents by Cause[a], 1983 - 1988

	Alaska		48-States	
	Fatal (%)	Nonfatal (%)	Fatal (%)	Nonfatal (%)
Equipment Failure	4	10	12	20
Seat Belt	0	0	0	0
Environment	5	12	4	8
Pilot Error	55	69	64	65
Air Traffic Control	b	b	b	b
Ground Crew	b	b	b	b
Other Aircraft	7	2	3	2
Company Operations	0	0	0	0
Other	30	7	1	4
Number of Accidents	104	803	2,435	9,972
Accidents per 100,000 hours	2.0	14.6	1.8	7.2

[a]Totals may not add to 100 percent due to rounding.
[b]Less than 1 percent.

Source: NTSB, *1986 Annual Report*; NTSB accident data tapes; U.S. Department of Transportation Federal Aviation Administration, Office of Management Systems, Management Standards and Statistics Division, *General Aviation Activity and Avionics Survey, Annual Summary Report*, assorted years.

proportion of accidents where the aircraft is not recovered or where the accident is not observed and the cause cannot be known with certainty.

PILOT ERROR AND SAFETY PERFORMANCE

Clearly, pilot error is the primary cause of general aviation accidents. It is a major factor in other aviation accidents as well. However, when all segments of the U.S. aviation industry are compared, a clear pattern of pilot error accidents across the industry emerges (Figure 3.4). It is important to remember that these are "unforced"

Figure 3.4   The Role of Pilot Error, Domestic U.S. Aviation Industry, 1979-1988

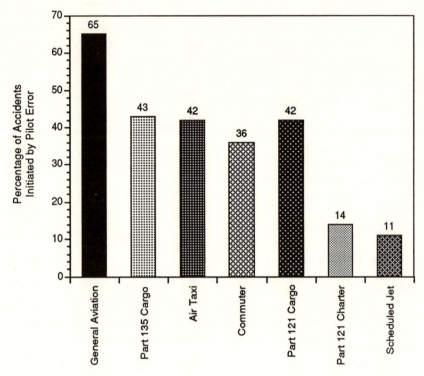

Source: Derived from NTSB Accident Data

pilot errors—those where the pilot's mistake started the sequence of events that led to the accident. As can be seen in Figure 3.4, there is a clear progression in the role of pilot error as one moves from general aviation, where it is highest at 65 percent, to cargo and nonscheduled passenger service, and finally to scheduled passenger service. The progression is similar in both the propeller portion of the industry (Part 135) and the jet portion of the industry (Part 121).

There would appear to be three factors behind this pattern: experience, licensing, and aptitude. While there are certainly some exceptions in terms of both company and pilot preferences, it is typically the case that professional pilots prefer employment with a scheduled jet airline. One common path is through military training with a pilot moving directly from the military to scheduled jet service. Increasingly, however, the more common path is a progression through the civilian ranks. Here, a pilot starts in the general aviation category for initial training and a private pilot's license. As the pilot gains experience and additional training, multiengine training and a commercial license are obtained. At this point, cargo and air taxis are an option for a pilot to build experience. With additional experience, a pilot may then move to scheduled commuter service and obtain an ATP rating. At that point, a move to a scheduled jet carrier is a possibility.

Throughout this career progression, the pilot is building experience and meeting stricter licensing requirements. Moreover, flying an airplane shares a characteristic with most other activities in that some people simply have more aptitude for it than do others. Not all pilots with equal experience and license ratings are equally skilled. Each employment stage also serves as a filter where the better pilots are most likely to move on to the next stage while those with less aptitude either stay at that level or leave the profession.

In the 1986-1988 period, pilots were drawn at an increasing rate from the commuter industry into the jet carrier industry to meet growing demand for air travel. To fill their pilot vacancies, commuters drew pilots from the air taxi and Part 135 cargo segments at a faster rate than they did previously. Some in the commuter industry expressed concern that fewer less-capable pilots were being filtered out in this accelerated process. While the overall commuter passenger fatality rate in 1986-1988 was only 30 percent of the rate for the 1979-1985 period, the pilot error rate in the later period was six times higher and accounted for almost all commuter fatalities. The rates at which pilots progress from one industry segment to another would appear to warrant close scrutiny if air safety is to be maintained or improved.

Some insights into the role of pilot error in aviation safety have been gained by placing the scheduled airline experience in the context of the nonscheduled and general aviation segments of the industry. Further insights into these risk tiers can be gained by extending the analysis to aviation safety outside the United States. The next chapter begins this extension by comparing U.S. aviation safety with that in Canada.

Chapter 4

A Comparison of Aviation Safety in Canada and the United States

How does aviation safety in the United States compare with safety elsewhere in the world? Canada provides a good starting point for comparison since Canadian aviation is more like U.S. aviation than is any other country. Both countries offer similar flight environments in terms of the mix of flight lengths, equipment, and airports and airways. Both countries use similar methods in maintaining accident investigation and airline operations data, thereby allowing detailed comparisons. Moreover, both countries have recently changed the economic regulatory environment under which their airlines operate. This changing economic environment has heightened concern about the level of safety in passenger air travel in Canada as well as in the United States.

Both the Canadian and U.S. airline industries contain a mix of carriers with widely differing characteristics ranging from large jet carriers to charter operators using very small single-engine planes. Care must be taken to ensure that similar industry segments in the two countries are being compared. Highly aggregated safety statistics can provide misleading comparisons of aviation safety between countries if they encompass markedly different types of carriers. To provide insight, analysis of aviation safety must control for varying stage lengths, different mixes of equipment, the variety of airports served, varied maintenance requirements and practices, and differing training and operating procedures.

This chapter begins by examining safety rates within the U.S. and Canadian industries and between comparable segments of these industries. Not surprisingly, the safety performance of these different types of carriers varies as widely within Canada as it does within the United States. Next, the distribution of accident causes in each segment of the Canadian and U.S. industries is analyzed and compared. Finally, the safety performance of the Canadian industry is compared to other operations worldwide.

SELECTING COMPARABLE INDUSTRY SEGMENTS

Table 4.1 presents selected operating characteristics of the Canadian Level 1, Level 2, and Level 3 carriers used in the comparison.[1] Level 1 carriers are most comparable to scheduled jet carriers operating under Part 121 in the United States. Within Level 1 there is considerable variation. The largest Level 1 carrier, Air Canada, is roughly comparable in passenger volume to Southwest Airlines. The other Level 1 carriers are substantially smaller than Air Canada and correspond in passenger volume to smaller U.S. jet carriers such as Midway and Aloha Airlines, or to the very largest U.S. commuter carriers such as Air Wisconsin, which operates both small jets and larger turboprops under Part 121 regulations.

Level 2 carriers are most comparable to mid-size U.S. commuters. There is considerable variation in size within Level 2, but the average Level 2 carrier would rank among the largest twenty U.S. commuters, in terms of enplanements. A carrier with enplanements that were the average of Level 3 carriers would rank about thirtieth in size among U.S. commuter airlines. Again, there is considerable size variation within Level 3; two of the carriers would rank near the top twenty U.S. carriers and two others out of the top fifty. In both the Canadian and U.S. industries, data are most complete and reliable for the large carriers.

In addition to the carriers reflected in the table, there are other important segments of the Canadian industry. Canadian Specific Point Service is most comparable to U.S. commuter service, particularly as offered by some of the smaller commuter carriers. Canadian charter and contract service is most comparable to U.S. Part 135 nonscheduled service. Other commercial services in

---

[1]Appendix C contains a list of the Canadian carriers in each group.

Table 4.1 Operations Characteristics of Canadian Carriers, 1983-1988

	Level 1 Carriers	Level 2 Carriers	Level 3 Carriers
Average Passengers per Flight	65	13	10
Average Minutes per Flight	102	48	67
Enplanements	151,353,859	16,520,031	1,923,717
Aircraft Departures	2,336,181	1,257,578	185,990
Flight Hours	3,969,238	1,007,733	207,791
Carriers in 1983	7	8	2
Carriers in 1988	4	7	4
Average 1988 Enplanements per Carrier	6,396,252	564,910	230,846

Source: Derived from data provided by Statistics Canada.

Canada find their closest counterpart in some segments of general aviation (Part 91) in the U.S., particularly with fixed-base operators.

COMPARING SAFETY PERFORMANCE

Table 4.2 compares Canadian Level 1 carriers with U.S. jet carriers using three measures of safety performance: total accidents (fatal and nonfatal) per 1 million aircraft departures, fatalities per 1 million enplanements, and serious injuries per 1 million enplanements. The Canadian carriers' safety record is significantly worse for accident and injury rates, and slightly lower (but not significantly different, statistically) for fatalities per 1 million enplanements.

Before attempting to draw conclusions from these differences, several things must be kept in mind. Nonfatal accidents are rare events in these segments of aviation in both the U.S. and Canada, and fatal accidents are even more uncommon. Between 1983 and 1988, there was only one fatal accident among Canadian Level 1 carriers, an in-flight fire on an Air Canada DC-9 in which 23 people were killed. That was a situation, like many in aviation, where there was a thin line between a nonfatal accident and an

Table 4.2 Comparing Canadian and U.S. Safety Performance, Canadian Level 1 and U.S. Jet Carriers

	Canadian Level 1 Carriers[a]	U.S. Jet Carriers
Total Accidents per 1 Million Departures	7.70	2.64[b]
Fatalities per 1 Million Enplanements	0.15	0.27
Injuries per 1 Million Enplanements	0.56	0.05[b]

[a]Canadian figures are for the 1983-1988 period and U.S. figures are for the 1979-1988 period.
[b]U.S. Jet Carrier rate is lower than Canadian Level 1 Carrier rate at the 95 percent confidence level.

Source: Canadian figures derived from data provided by the CASB and Statistics Canada. U.S. figures derived from data provided by the NTSB and the FAA.

accident where all passengers are killed. Had the fire progressed further prior to landing, the Air Canada accident could easily have killed everyone on board. Conversely, had the fire not started or had it started during a different portion of the flight, there might have been no fatalities. In another incident that same year, an Air Canada B-767 ran out of fuel over western Canada, but, was able to land without any fatalities through pilot skill and considerable good fortune in being able to find an abandoned air field in this sparsely settled region. That situation could have easily ended in an accident with many fatalities. The point of these examples is that fatality rates, as well as accident rates, can vary substantially from year to year because of the unique circumstances surrounding each accident.

In many respects, the rate of total accidents per 1 million departures is the most revealing of the three measures in Table 4.2. The number of fatalities or injuries in an accident can often be a matter of chance, including how many passengers boarded that particular flight, and as a result, there is considerable year-to-year variation in fatality and injury rates. The accident rate, however, shows considerably less variation and may well present a better measure of safety for comparisons made over short periods of time.

Focusing on accident rates, Canadian Level 1 safety performance is appreciably worse than that of U.S. jet carriers. Not only is the

Canadian average in Table 4.2 higher, but, as Figure 4.1 shows, the rates in each year are consistently higher as well. Figure 4.1 shows the U.S. rate for 1980-1988 and the Level 1 rate for 1983-1988. The U.S. rate is based on far more departures and shows far less year-to-year variation. The Canadian rate shows more variation, but is still higher than the U.S. rate for all but one of the years shown. The examination of accident causes, discussed later in this section, looks at possible reasons for differences in safety performance of jet carriers in the two countries.

Table 4.3 compares the safety performance of Canadian Level 2 carriers with that of the largest twenty U.S. commuter airlines. For U.S. commuters, reliable aircraft departure data are not available, so only fatality and injury rates can be calculated and compared. As can be seen in the table, the Canadian and U.S. carriers have about the same fatality rates, while the U.S. carriers appear to have slightly lower serious injury rates. The safety performances of these two segments, thus, seem quite similar.

The data also suggest that the relative safety performance of different industry segments is similar in the U.S. and Canada. In comparing Tables 4.2 and 4.3, the Level 2 fatality rate is three times the Level 1 rate and the U.S. large commuter rate is nearly twice the jet carrier rate. These differences are not surprising. In the United States, for example, as one moves from general aviation to charter to commuter service to jet carrier service, several things

Figure 4.1 Canadian and U.S. Jet Carrier Accident Rates, 1983-1988

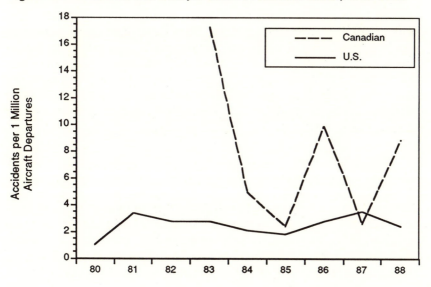

Table 4.3 Comparing Canadian and U.S. Safety Performance, Canadian Level 2 and U.S. Top Twenty Commuters

	Canadian Level 2 Carriers[a]	U.S. Top Twenty Commuters
Accidents per 1 Million Departures	15.11	NA[b]
Fatalities per 1 Million Enplanements	0.48	0.41
Injuries per 1 Million Enplanements	0.54	0.19

[a]Canadian figures are for the 1983-1988 period and U.S. figures are for the 1979-1988 period.
[b]NA - Reliable aircraft departure data are not available for U.S. commuter carriers.

Source: Canadian figures derived from data provided by the CASB and Statistics Canada. U.S. figures derived from data provided by the NTSB and the FAA.

that can influence safety change systematically. First, as discussed in the previous chapter, pilots typically have more experience and must meet stricter licensing standards. Second, aircraft become more sophisticated with more redundancy and better backup systems. Third, flights operate into airports with longer runways and better landing aids.

Table 4.4 compares the safety performance of the Canadian Level 3 carriers with that of medium-size U.S. commuters, those ranked twenty-first through fiftieth, and small U.S. commuters ranked smaller than the top fifty. Both Canadian Level 3 carriers and U.S. small commuters are substantially less safe than larger commuter carriers. Also, the Canadian performance falls between that of the two U.S. industry segments. Again, this is not surprising since this portion of the Canadian industry is made up both of carriers similar to medium U.S. commuters and of carriers similar to small U.S. commuters.

CAUSES OF AVIATION ACCIDENTS

The following analyses of the distribution of causes in Canadian accidents are based on an examination of 794 commercial service accidents of fixed wing aircraft between 1983 and 1988. For some of the accidents in 1988 and a few in 1987, cause could not be assigned because the Canadian Air Safety Board (CASB) had not

Table 4.4 Comparing Canadian and U.S. Safety Performance, Canadian Level 3, U.S. Commuters Ranked Twenty-one Through Fifty, and U.S. Commuters Ranked Fifty-one and Higher

	Canadian Level 3 Carriers[a]	U.S. 21-50 Commuters	U.S. 51+ Commuters
Accidents per 1 Million Departures	48.40	NA[b]	NA[b]
Fatalities per 1 Million Enplanements	2.08	0.84[c]	4.19
Injuries per 1 Million Enplanements	1.04	0.49[c]	2.54

[a]Canadian figures are for the 1983-1988 period and U.S. figures are for the 1979-1988 period.
[b]NA - Reliable aircraft departure data is not available for U.S. commuter carriers.
[c]The U.S. Commuters Ranked Twenty-one Through Fifty rate is lower than the U.S. Commuters Ranked Fifty-one and Higher rate at the 95 percent confidence level.

Source: Canadian figures derived from data provided by the CASB and Statistics Canada. U.S. figures derived from data provided by the NTSB and the FAA.

finished its investigation of the accident. The analysis of the distribution of causes in U.S. accidents is based on a total of 14,011 accidents.[2] Each accident was placed in one of the nine major cause categories used in the previous two chapters.[3]

Table 4.5 provides a comparison of the distribution of accident causes for Canadian scheduled commercial service with U.S. scheduled Part 121 service. The service provided in these two segments is similar, with perhaps a slightly greater portion of the Canadian service provided in large turboprop aircraft. The U.S. scheduled Part 121 service also contains some service by turboprops operated by predominantly jet carriers as well as some provided by large commuters operating under Part 121. As can be seen in this table and those that follow, environment and pilot error are the most common causes of accidents in Canada.

There are noticeable differences between the two distributions shown in Table 4.5, but they must be interpreted with caution because the Canadian distribution is based on only ten accidents. The largest apparent differences are that equipment failure and

[2]The breakdown of these accidents is indicated in Tables 4.5 through 4.9.
[3]For accidents involving ski-equipped aircraft landing on snow or ice, the accident was considered weather if the pilot took reasonable precautions to insure the surface was suitable for operation.

Table 4.5 Comparison of the Distribution of Accident Causes, Canadian Scheduled Commercial Service and U.S. Scheduled Jet Service[a]

	Canadian[b] (%)	U.S. (%)
Equipment	10	20
Seatbelt	0	24
Environment	40	19
Pilot Error	30	11
Air Traffic Control	0	6
Ground Crew	10	7
Other Aircraft	0	2
Company Operations	0	2
Other	10	9
Number of Accidents	10	115

[a]Domestic and international service is included for both countries. Totals may not add to 100 percent due to rounding.
[b]Canadian figures are for the 1983-1988 period and U.S. figures are for the 1979-1988 period.

Source: Canadian figures derived from data provided by the CASB. U.S. figures derived from data provided by the NTSB.

seatbelt not fastened are proportionately more important in the United States, whereas environment and pilot error are proportionately more important in Canadian operations. While the Canadian distribution is based on only 10 accidents, it is, nevertheless, interesting that there were no injuries reported from not wearing a seatbelt, a relatively common source of injury in U.S. jet service.

The share of accidents by cause in Table 4.5 can be combined with the accident rates reported in Table 4.2 to calculate accident rates by cause. Table 4.6 contains these accident rates for four major categories: equipment, environment, pilot error, and all other. As can be seen, the environment and pilot error rates are dramatically higher in Canada while the equipment and all other rates are about the same for Canada and the United States. Virtually all of the difference between the safety of these Canadian and U.S. segments is accounted for by higher rates of pilot error and environment accidents in Canada.

Table 4.7 compares Canadian Specific Point Service with U.S. scheduled service in the forty-eight-state region and in Alaska. The service provided by Canadian Specific Point Service is in a flight environment intermediate between that found in the continental U.S. and in Alaska. Much Canadian service is like that in the forty-eight-state region involving flights between

Table 4.6 Comparison of Accident Rates by Cause, Canadian Level 1 Carriers and U.S. Scheduled Jet Carriers[a]

	Canadian[b]	U.S.
Equipment	0.77	0.53
Environment	3.08	0.50[c]
Pilot Error	2.31	0.29[c]
Other	1.54	1.32
Total	7.70	2.64[c]

[a]Total accidents per 1 million departures.
[b]Canadian figures are for the 1983-1988 period and U.S. figures are for the 1979-1988 period.
[c]The U.S. rate is lower than the Canadian rate at the 95 percent confidence level.

Source: Derived from data contained in Tables 4.2 and 4.5.
Canadian figures derived from data provided by the CASB and Statistics Canada.
U.S. figures derived from data provided by the NTSB and the FAA.

Table 4.7 Comparison of the Distribution of Accident Causes, Canadian Specific Point Commercial Service and U.S. Scheduled Part 135 Service

	Canadian[a] (%)	U.S. 48-State (%)	U.S. Alaska (%)
Equipment	37	30	18
Seatbelt	0	1	0
Environment	22	14	16
Pilot Error	41	36	51
Air Traffic Control	0	1	2
Ground Crew	0	10	2
Other Aircraft	0	4	4
Company	0	1	0
Other	0	2	7
Number of Accidents	27	140	45

[a]Canadian figures are for the 1983-1988 period and U.S. figures are for the 1979-1988 period. Totals may not add to 100 percent due to rounding.

Source: Canadian figures derived from data provided by the CASB.
U.S. figures derived from data provided by the NTSB.

reasonably well-equipped airports. Other service is more like Alaska, where some flights serve airports with nonpaved runways or use float-equipped or ski-equipped aircraft. Perhaps it is not surprising, then, that the role of pilot error in this Canadian segment falls between that in the forty-eight states and that in Alaska. It is surprising, however, that the share of environment accidents is higher than either in the continental U.S. or in Alaska. In addition, the Canadian Specific Point Service also has a greater share of equipment failure accidents. Here, the explanation may be that carriers providing Canadian Specific Point Service appear to use a higher proportion of piston-powered as opposed to turboprop aircraft.

Table 4.8 compares Canadian charter commercial service with U.S. Part 135 charter service in both the forty-eight-state region and in Alaska. As can be seen in the table, the mix of Canadian causes is very similar to those found in Alaska even though many of the accidents occurred in flight environments most like the continental U.S.. Pilot error accidents for Canadian charters are more frequent than in the forty-eight-states and occur at about the same frequency as in Alaska. Table 4.9 compares the distribution of accident causes for other Canadian commercial service with U.S. general aviation in both the forty-eight-states and in Alaska. These three distributions are based on the largest number of accidents of any of the tables and are very similar.

Figure 4.2 compares the proportion of pilot error in aviation accidents for Canadian and U.S. carriers across the four segments.

Table 4.8 Comparison of the Distribution of Accident Causes, Canadian Charter Commercial Service and U.S. Charter Part 135 Service

	Canadian[a] (%)	U.S. 48-State (%)	U.S. Alaska (%)
Equipment	23	29	16
Seatbelt	0	0	0
Environment	14	9	13
Pilot Error	55	43	54
Air Traffic Control	0	0	0
Ground Crew	2	2	0
Other Aircraft	1	5	3
Company	0	1	0
Other	6	11	15
Number of Accidents	313	312	114

[a]Canadian figures are for the 1983-1988 period and U.S. figures are for the 1983-1988 period. Totals may not add to 100 percent due to rounding.

Source: Canadian figures derived from data provided by the CASB.
U.S. figures derived from data provided by the NTSB.

Table 4.9 Comparison of the Distribution of Accident Causes, Other Canadian Commercial Service and U.S. General Aviation

	Canadian[a] (%)	U.S. 48-State (%)	U.S. Alaska (%)
Equipment	17	19	9
Seatbelt	0	0	0
Environment	7	7	12
Pilot Error	70	65	67
ATC	b	b	b
Ground Crew	b	b	b
Other Aircraft	1	3	2
Company	0	0	0
Other	4	6	9
Number of Accidents	444	12,407	907

[a]Canadian figures are for the 1983-1988 period and U.S. figures are for the 1983-1988 period. Totals may not add to 100 percent due to rounding.
[b]Less than 1 percent.

Source: Canadian figures derived from data provided by the CASB and U.S. figures derived from data provided by the NTSB.

Figure 4.2 The Role of Pilot Error in Aviation Accidents

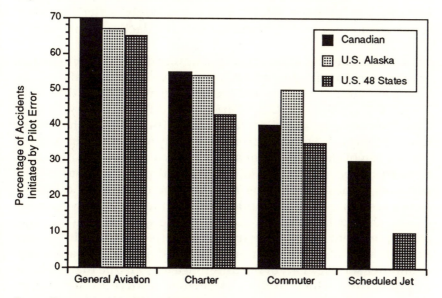

Source: Derived from CASB and NTSB data.

Several patterns emerge in the figure. The most notable pattern is that in all three industry segments the proportion of pilot error drops as one moves from general aviation to charter to commuter to scheduled jet. A second pattern is that the drop in the share of pilot error is less pronounced in the Canadian and Alaskan segments than it is in the U.S. forty-eight-states. The difference is most pronounced in comparing U.S. and Canadian scheduled jet service. (Alaska scheduled jet service is not distinguishable from that in the rest of the U.S. and is not presented separately.)

In the continental U.S., the drop in the proportion (and rate) of pilot error accidents in moving from general aviation to charter to commuter to jet carrier is not surprising. As discussed in Chapter 3, the decline in pilot error mirrors the career progressions of many pilots, starting in general aviation where initial flight instruction and licensing takes place; obtaining a commercial license after more training and experience; moving to charter service; moving to commuter service, where an ATP license is obtained; and finally moving to scheduled jet service. In addition to higher levels of experience, a filtering process takes place as pilots progress from level to level with better pilots selected by the carriers to move on to the next level while less skilled pilots remain at lower levels or leave the profession. An alternate career path in the United States is to receive initial flight training and experience in military service and move directly to commuters or more likely to jet service. The increase in training, experience, filtering out of poor pilots, and increasingly strict licensing requirements appears to produce a steadily declining proportion of pilot error as an initiator of accidents.

As the figure illustrates, there is a similar drop in the proportion of pilot error in Canadian and Alaskan service, but the differences between segments are less and the levels remain higher than they do for the continental U.S. Part of the difference may be that Canadian and Alaskan pilots face more difficult flying challenges than do their U.S. counterparts. It certainly appears that a greater proportion of these operations are conducted on ski-equipped or float-equipped aircraft or to and from airports without paved runways. These operations may be inherently more difficult, with a resulting increase in pilot error accidents. However, these effects should be confined largely to the general aviation and charter segments of the industry and do not explain the differences in the share of pilot error in scheduled jet or perhaps even commuter service. Part of the difference may also be that the base of pilots from which to draw is smaller relative to demand in Alaska and Canada than in the continental U.S. If so, there may be less filtering out of less skilled pilots as pilots progress from segment to segment.

CANADIAN AIR SAFETY IN THE CONTEXT OF WORLDWIDE OPERATIONS

While Canadian Level 1 carriers had a worse safety record during the mid-late 1980s than did their U.S. counterparts, Canadian carriers compare favorably with most of the world's airlines. As discussed in the next chapter in more detail, international comparisons are difficult because of erratic reporting of both accidents and operations data and because of differing standards regarding what gets reported. Thus, it is best to focus on fatal accident rates, where underreporting and differing definitions are least likely to be a problem. Even here, the rates presented must be interpreted as indicating broad differences only.

Taken together, the Canadian Level 1, 2, and 3 carriers had, on average, a fatal accident approximately every 764,000 aircraft departures during 1983-1988. Comparable figures can be calculated for other regions of the world by aggregating the safety records of scheduled airlines, including both international and domestic jet carriers and commuters. Looking at the 1977-1989 period, Canadian carriers had slightly better performances than did Western European carriers as a group, who experienced a fatal accident every 870,000 departures. Elsewhere in the world, however, air safety performance was dramatically worse. Eastern European carriers had a fatal accident every 243,000 departures; Asian carriers every 215,000 departures; Middle Eastern carriers every 183,000 departures; Latin American carriers every 166,000 departures; and African carriers every 75,000 departures.

The next chapter expands the international aviation safety comparison by examining the comparative safety performance of domestic and international operations for flag carriers and domestic airlines worldwide.

Chapter 5

The International
Safety Record

As international travel has grown, the extent to which citizens of one country fly on airlines of other nations is at an all time high. Any assessment of aviation safety worldwide must go beyond merely comparing safety records of international flag carriers that fly relatively long flights between major airports to examine flights within countries as well. Furthermore, the globalization of the airline industry has led to a growing number of marketing agreements, operational ties, and cross-ownership relations. Since these organizational links are intended (in part) to capture passenger traffic, the comparative safety performance of potential airline partners has become an important management and public policy issue.

DATA LIMITATIONS

Information on international airline operations and safety is not as comprehensive as that for the United States, Canada, or even most of Western Europe. The International Civil Aviation Organization (ICAO), based in Montreal, collects data and conducts accident and incident analyses for member countries. As of 1988, there were 92 member nations in ICAO, representing 146 international scheduled airlines, 60 domestic scheduled airlines, and 26 charter operators. The safety-related activities of ICAO concentrate on conducting safety studies, making recommendations, and helping less-developed nations bring their airline, airport, and air traffic control facilities and operating practices to world standards.

Safety data collected by ICAO is known as the Accident/ Incident Reporting (ADREP) System. The ADREP system dates back only to 1977, making it difficult to analyze historical safety performance over the long term. A bigger problem, however, is the lack of current data. The ADREP annual statistics and corresponding accident summaries appear with a lag of about four years. This lengthy delay occurs because initial data reporting from some nations is inconsistent and often sketchy, which then requires substantial follow-up effort to obtain more reliable data. As of early 1991, the most recent publicly available ICAO ADREP safety data covered 1986.

However, information on international airline safety is available from other aviation publications. *Flight International* provides an annual summary of fatal and nonfatal accidents for the world's airlines and includes information on date, airline, aircraft, fatalities, passengers, and a brief summary of the accident. For this analysis, information was supplemented by reports on each accident available in other aviation publications, including *Aviation Week and Space Technology, Air Transport World, Interavia,* and information from trade associations. To evaluate the accuracy of these various data, the information was compared with that produced by ICAO's ADREP system for the 1977-1986 period. The data from *Flight International* report a slightly higher number of accidents over the period, with little year-to-year variation. Virtually all the accidents in the ICAO ADREP data appear in the *Flight International* series; the only noteworthy exceptions (with regard to fatal accidents) are accidents in the Soviet Union and the People's Republic of China.[1] Thus, although some reporting biases and some differences in numbers remain, the available data allow assessment of the international aviation safety record.[2]

---

[1]Other studies have not included the Soviet Union because of apparent underreporting or because of imprecise estimates of traffic or passenger data. Those problems notwithstanding, even the incomplete data help assess the relative safety performance of Aeroflot in the Soviet Union. Unfortunately, no traffic data is available for CAAC, the airline of the People's Republic of China.

[2]For a review of the prior safety records of international flag carriers, see A. Barnett, M. Abraham, and V. Schimmel,"Airline Safety: Some Empirical Findings," *Management Science* 25 (1979): 1045-56. A more recent update is provided by A. Barnett and M. Higgins, "Airline Safety: The Last Decade," *Management Science* 35 (January 1989): 1-21.

THE SAFETY RECORD OF SCHEDULED AIRLINES

How safe have the world's airlines been? Table 5.1 shows that worldwide fatal accident rates have declined over the past thirty years. In terms of the probability of being involved in a plane crash in which at least some people die, the probability had declined nearly 50 percent from approximately 4.5 in 1 million in the early 1960s to approximately 2.4 in 1 million in the 1980s. Table 5.2 shows the number of fatal accidents and fatalities reported by ICAO involving scheduled airlines by year between 1977 and 1986. During that time, ICAO reports 233 fatal accidents that killed 7,404 people. However, these data cover only ICAO member countries. *Flight International* provides a more comprehensive account; Table 5.3 shows that between 1977 and 1989, there were 333 fatal accidents that killed 13,008 people.

To make comparisons between carriers, across regions, or over time, the number of accidents and fatalities must be converted to safety rates. As in the United States and Canada, the vast majority of accidents worldwide occur during the takeoff/climb or approach/landing phases so that a departure-based measure would be preferred. The logical choice is to use flight departures as the unit of risk exposure. However, because aircraft size and load factors vary widely across airlines, simple measures of fatalities per 100,000 aircraft departures do not permit meaningful comparisons.

To develop useful comparisons in light of these data limitations, one must distinguish an accident that kills all passengers aboard from a crash where a small number die. "Fatal accidents" include all occurrences in which a passenger or crew member dies. One such accident involved a China Airways B-747 that encountered severe turbulence near Hong Kong on August 16, 1982. Two

Table 5.1 Historical Fatal Accident Rate, Worldwide, Excluding the Soviet Union and China

Years	Fatal Accidents per 1 Million Departures
1957-1966	4.44
1967-1976	3.09
1977-1989	2.37

Source: Compiled from data in ICAO, *Traffic: Commercial Air Carriers*, various years; ICAO, *Accident/Incident Reporting (ADREP) Annual Statistics*, various years; *Flight International*, Annual Review of Safety, various issues.

Table 5.2   Accidents and Fatalities, Scheduled Airline Service, 1977-1986

Airplanes Over 27,000 kg (Jet Aircraft)

Year	Number of Accidents Fatal	Nonfatal	Number of Fatalities	Number of Aircraft Destroyed
1977	13	31	493	13
1978	13	34	606	13
1979	14	33	781	14
1980	10	31	696	10
1981	10	34	173	7
1982	12	31	481	15
1983	13	40	787	16
1984	4	26	57	6
1985	8	31	1,195	6
1986	9	45	459	6
Total	106	336	6,028	106

Airplanes Between 2,250 - 27,000 kg (Turboprop Aircraft)

Year	Fatal	Nonfatal	Fatalities	Destroyed
1977	15	44	108	21
1978	8	17	100	8
1979	18	22	161	18
1980	9	19	112	11
1981	13	16	158	14
1982	16	34	239	19
1983	8	28	42	10
1984	13	22	148	12
1985	17	29	211	24
1986	10	28	97	11
Total	127	259	1,376	148

Source: ICAO, *Accident/Incident Reporting (ADREP) Annual Statistics*, various years. Data available only through 1986 due to reporting, investigative, and publication lags; the 1986 statistics were published in December 1989. Data limited to ICAO member countries.

passengers not wearing seatbelts were killed. While this event certainly was tragic, the risk of injury to passengers wearing their seatbelts was far less than in other fatal accidents. Thus, both the probability of a fatal accident and the likelihood of being killed if such an accident occurred must be taken into account, particularly in light of continuing efforts to improve the survivability of airline crashes.

Table 5.3 Worldwide Safety Record by Year,ᵃ 1977-1989

Year	Number of Fatal Accidents	Number of Fatalities	Percentage of Passengers Killed in Crash	Fatal Accidents per 1 Million Departures	Death Risk per 1 Million Departures
1977	23	725	74	2.34	1.73
1978	26	859	59	2.58	1.52
1979	17	1085	74	1.68	1.24
1980	23	1047	65	2.24	1.46
1981	11	339	71	1.09	0.77
1982	27	946	70	2.68	1.87
1983	24	1197	69	2.32	1.60
1984	20	424	83	1.89	1.57
1985	26	1631	83	2.41	2.00
1986	29	721	59	2.59	1.53
1987	25	846	81	2.13	1.73
1988	38	1466	63	3.09	1.94
1989	44	1722	59	3.44	2.01
1977-1989	333	13,008	68	2.37	1.61
1977-1982	127	5,001	68	2.10	1.42
1983-1989	206	8,007	69	2.59	1.78

ᵃIncludes scheduled and nonscheduled passenger flights, regional/commuter operations, and occurrences involving sabotage, hijack, or military action against civilian targets. Fatalities include crew members.

Source: Compiled from *Flight International*, various issues; ICAO, *Traffic Statistics*, various issues.

The basic measures used here to evaluate risk are the number of fatal accidents per million flight departures, and the measure of the "death risk" per million departures. Death risk is the probability of being involved in a fatal accident multiplied by the proportion of people killed in fatal accidents. In short, this measures the probability of being in a crash in which some people die, and the chances of being killed in such a crash.[3]

Constructing these measures is useful for two reasons. First, such measures reflect an aggregate level of safety, providing information about comparative safety performance—how much more risky it has been to fly in Africa, say, than in Western Europe—regardless of why the safety records are different. Second, such estimates serve as a useful starting point for more detailed analysis of why safety performance varies so much across carriers, nations, and regions.

Table 5.3 shows the worldwide safety record for 1977-1989 as compiled from *Flight International* and other industry sources. The first three columns give the year, the number of fatal crashes, and the number of fatalities. The fourth column gives the average percentage of passengers killed in these fatal accidents. The fifth column in the table shows the odds per 1 million flight departures of being involved in an accident in which someone is killed. The final column gives the resulting chances per 1 million flight departures of an individual passenger being killed in airline travel. As shown at the bottom of the table, the safety record appears to have deteriorated between 1977-1982 and 1983-1989, although the difference was not statistically significant. Also, the table provides no support for the hypothesis that crash survivability is improving worldwide. As one might expect, given the U.S. and Canadian experiences reported in preceding chapters, the year-to-year variations in all of these measures are quite large.

Table 5.4 shows the airline safety record in the major geographic regions of the world. As in Table 5.3, the last two columns of Table 5.4 give the chances in 1 million departures of being involved in a fatal accident and of being killed on a flight in each region from 1977 to 1988. There is considerable variation among regions. For the United States and Canada, the chance of being killed was less than 0.6 in 1 million, the best safety record of any region.[4] The safety record in Western Europe also was excellent, with chances of being killed in a plane crash less than one in a million. Australia and New Zealand also produced exemplary safety records. Unfortunately, safety performance is markedly worse in the rest of the world. The chances of being killed in a plane crash in

---

[3]A more detailed discussion of these measures is found in Appendix A.

[4]These numbers differ from those of Barnett and Higgins. Their data cover 1977-1986, and are presented separately for domestic and international operations. Also, the United States experienced several fatal crashes in 1987 and 1988. These included fatal accidents involving Continental, Northwest, Delta, Pan Am, and USAir (through its PSA operations).

Table 5.4. Accident and Fatality Record by Region, Scheduled Passenger Flights,[a] 1977-1989

Region	Number of Fatal Accidents	Number of Fatalities	Percent of Passengers Killed in Crash	Fatal Accidents per 1 Million Departures	Death Risk per 1 Million Departures
North America	63	1971	60	0.88[b]	0.53[c]
Latin America	64	2326	81	6.04	4.87
Western Europe	30	1663	70	1.15	0.80
Eastern Europe	33	1662	62	4.11	2.53
Asia	63	2439	64	4.66	2.97
Africa	31	1110	79	13.25	10.52
Middle East	17	1373	69	5.47	3.78
Australia/ New Zealand	5	33	81	1.34	1.09

[a]Does not include regional and commuter operations.
[b]The North American rate is lower than the Latin American, Eastern European, Asian, African, and Middle Eastern rates at the 95 percent confidence level.
[c]The North American rate is lower than the Eastern European rate at the 90 percent confidence level and the Latin American, Asian, African, and Middle Eastern rates at the 95 percent confidence level.

Source: Compiled from *Flight International, Aviation Week and Space Technology, Air Transport World, Interavia*, and ICAO, ADREP, various years.

Eastern Europe and Asia were 4.8 and 5.6 times worse, respectively, than North America. The Middle East and Latin America were 7.1 and 9.2 times worse. Africa had the worst safety record, with a death risk per flight of nearly 10.5 per 1 million, almost twenty times worse than in North America.[5]

The relative regional performances do not change much when comparing the 1977-1982 and 1983-1988 periods. The rank order of safety performance stays the same. However, there were slight increases in fatal accident rates in North America and the Middle East, and small improvements in Africa, Asia, and Western Europe. It is important to understand what data lie behind the construction of Table 5.4. First, the table includes all domestic and international

[5]It is possible to test statistically the differences among regions. However, the use of such statistical tests is open to question, since these data reflect the *ex post* universe of accident performance of the world's airlines rather than a random sample of such performance.

scheduled flights by airlines based in the region. All reported jet, turboprop, and piston engine flights are included. The regional breakdowns in Table 5.4, thus, represent one attempt to examine the effect of differences in airline operating environments.

In addition to regional differences, one might expect larger carriers to have different safety records than smaller carriers. Table 5.5 divides 162 airlines into four departure categories. The largest class contains airlines with over 1 million flights between 1977 and 1989. This represents an average of over 200 flights per day. For comparison purposes, all the major U.S. airlines fall in this category; carriers just meeting this threshold include Varig of Brazil and Japan Airlines. Two thirds of the total flights are in this first group. The second category, 500,000 to 1 million departures, includes most Western European carriers. Airlines just meeting the 500,000-flight threshold include JAT (Yugoslavia) and Aloha in the United States. The 100,000-500,000 departures category includes smaller carriers such as Aer Lingus, Aero Boliviano, and Singapore Airlines.

The table shows a marked increase in fatal accident rates as one moves from the largest carriers to the smallest. Since the world's air traffic is dominated by flights in North America and Western Europe, one might ask whether the relation between size

Table 5.5 Airline Accident Rates, Classified by Total Departures, 1977 - 1989

Airlines with:	Number of Airlines	Total Departures (millions)	Fatal Accidents per 1 Million Departures	Death Risk per 1 Million Departures
Over 1 million departures	28	80.753	0.82	0.50
500,000 to 1 million departures	30	22.031	1.63	1.11
100,000 to 500,000 departures	66	15.751	3.62[a]	2.56[a]
Less than 100,000 departures	38	1.697	8.84[a,b]	7.06[a,b]
All Groups	162	120.242	1.45	0.98

[a]The rate for the over 1 million departures category is lower at the 95 percent confidence level.
[b]The rate for the 500,000 to 1 million departures category is lower at the 95 percent confidence level.

Source: Compiled from *Flight International, Aviation Week and Space Technology, Air Transport World, Interavia*, and ICAO, ADREP, various years.

and safety is really just a proxy for regional differences. To address this question accident rates for large and small carriers *within* each region were calculated. The airlines were divided on the basis of median departures for airlines in that region. The results are shown in Table 5.6. As expected, the median departure figure varies substantially across regions. Within each region, though, larger carriers have fatal accident rates two to three times lower than that region's smaller airlines. The only exceptions are in Eastern Europe, in which Aeroflot's poor performance dominates the results, and in Africa, where smaller airlines have safety records six times worse than their larger counterparts in the region. Thus, both regional differences and variations in operating experience (as measured by the cumulative number of flights) are associated with quite divergent safety records worldwide.

It is difficult to determine whether the airline or the region is the principal source of safety risk. Unfortunately, it is not possible to construct safety rates by carrier by regional market. Thus, the available data do not permit a direct test of whether it has been safer to fly on, say, European carriers into Africa, than on African carriers. However, the accident record itself can be examined to see the proportions of accidents in each country that were accounted for by that country's own airlines, by other airlines in the same region, or by airlines from other regions of the world.

Sixty-eight percent of the fatal accidents between 1977 and 1989 involved an airline of the country in which the crash occurred. Another 14 percent of fatal crashes involved airlines in the same region. Only 18 percent of the fatal accidents involved airlines from another part of the world. Moreover, the overwhelming number of these cases were accidents in which a carrier from a developing region crashed either in Europe or in another developing area. Thus, while there is no direct evidence on safety performance of different airlines in the same markets, it does appear that the airlines of North America and Western Europe have better safety records flying in developing areas than the local airlines.

Another issue is the effect the type of aircraft operated by an airline has on its safety performance. As noted in earlier chapters, carriers operating smaller piston engine or turboprop aircraft in the United States have had safety records significantly worse than those of U.S. jet carriers. Because the carriers that report data to ICAO tend to be larger and operate at least some jet aircraft, a similar commuter-jet comparison cannot be made here. However, carriers reporting data to ICAO can be divided into those airlines with predominantly jet fleets versus those airlines in which at least 25 percent of their planes are piston or turboprop.

Table 5.6 Regional Variations in Death Risk per Flight, Large and Small Airlines,[a] 1977-1989

	Number of Airlines	Median Regional Departures (millions)	Fatal Accidents per 1 Million Departures	Death Risk per 1 Million Departures
North America				
Large			0.50	0.24
Small			1.34	0.72
Total	20	1.885	0.60	0.30
Latin America				
Large			3.11[b]	2.15[b]
Small			7.74	6.57
Total	36	0.147	3.74	2.76
Western Europe				
Large			0.50	0.34
Small			1.27	1.06
Total	32	0.576	0.62	0.45
Eastern Europe				
Large			2.90	2.28
Small			3.57	1.85
Total	6	0.429	2.97	2.24
Asia[d]				
Large			2.16	1.34[b]
Small			4.88	4.06
Total	27	0.308	2.59	1.77
Africa				
Large			3.20[b]	2.40[b]
Small			20.49	13.12
Total	21	0.060	5.67	3.95
Middle East				
Large			2.51[c]	1.68
Small			5.80	3.39
Total	13	0.176	3.25	2.07

[a]Large/small defined as above/below median number of departures for that region. Australia/New Zealand are not shown because of a lack of departure data for small carriers.
[b]The Large rate is lower than the Small rate at the 95 percent confidence level.
[c]The Large rate is lower than the Small rate at the 90 percent confidence level.
[d]Asia statistics do not include China Airlines, CAAC (People's Republic of China), and Burma Airways, all of which had multiple fatal accidents but for which departure data was unavailable.

Source: Compiled from Flight International, Aviation Week and Space Technology, Air Transport World, Interavia, and ICAO, ADREP, various years.

The safety records for these two segments by region are shown in Table 5.7. The table is incomplete because fleet data were not available to classify carriers for Eastern Europe and Africa. However, in Western Europe, Latin America, and Asia, the results found for the United States appear to hold as well; airlines that operate a substantial percentage of commuter aircraft have safety records between two and three times worse than those of predominantly jet carriers.

These aggregate safety records, however divergent, may still mask wide differences in safety records across individual airlines. Table 5.8 presents fatal accident rates for all carriers for which departure data were available from ICAO. Accident rates reflect all fatal accidents that were reported to ICAO or appeared in

Table 5.7 Comparison of Accident Rates by Region, Jet versus Mixed Fleet Carriers,[a] 1977-1989

	Fatal Accidents per 1 Million Departures	Death Risk per 1 Million Departures
Worldwide		
Predominantly Jet Fleet[b]	2.22	1.54
Mixed Fleet[c]	4.30	3.79
Western Europe		
Predominantly Jet Fleet	0.47	0.36
Mixed Fleet	1.41	1.33
Latin America		
Predominantly Jet Fleet	3.12	2.21[d]
Mixed Fleet	5.51	5.16
Asia		
Predominantly Jet Fleet	4.41	3.15
Mixed Fleet	6.02	5.10

[a]North America is excluded because the U.S. commuter airline safety record is examined in detail in Chapter 2 and the Canadian airline safety record is examined in detail in Chapter 4. Australia and New Zealand are excluded due to the absence of jet crashes and lack of information on commuter aircraft departures. Eastern Europe and Africa are omitted due to incomplete or missing fleet composition data.
[b]"Predominantly jet fleet" is defined as having more than 75 percent jet aircraft.
[c]"Mixed fleet" are those carriers with 25 percent or more of their fleet comprised of turboprop or piston engine aircraft. The relative performance is not affected if alternative percentage breakdowns are used.
[d]The Predominantly Jet Fleet rate is lower than the Mixed Fleet rate at the 90 percent confidence level.

Source: Compiled from *Flight International, Aviation Week and Space Technology, Air Transport World, Interavia,* and ICAO, ADREP, various years.

Flight International. Incomplete data also are presented for carriers that reported fatal accidents, but for which departure data were unavailable, such as Burma Airways and Alymeda (People's Republic of Yemen). The regional groupings in the table are not strictly comparable to either Table 5.4 or 5.6 because not all of each region's airlines are represented. In addition, the data for the Soviet Union are based on incomplete accident reports and ICAO-reported estimates of departures. Finally, it is important to reiterate that the data presented here reflect accident rates for prior years, and should be interpreted with caution. Caution is especially warranted for individual airline data, particularly for smaller carriers whose safety rates can be affected dramatically by one accident.

Table 5.8 shows that a large number of the world's airlines had no fatal accidents between 1977 and 1989. This group includes such prominent airlines as Aerolineas Argentinas, British Airways, SAS, Cathay Pacific, ANA, Singapore Airlines, Egyptair, and Qantas in addition to many small carriers. The list of airlines that did not experience fatal accidents is a bit misleading because it represents only scheduled domestic and international flights; there are a few airlines that did not have fatal accidents on scheduled flights, but did experience fatal crashes on charter flights. These carriers include Air France, Air New Zealand, Dan-Air (Britain), and KLM. The distinction is important because of the significant role charter service plays in international vacation travel. It should be recalled that the world's worst airline crash involved the on-ground collision of B-747s operated by KLM and Pan Am, that killed 583 persons. Both the KLM and Pan Am flights were nonscheduled charter service.

A second feature of Table 5.8, beyond the accident-free carriers, is that several airlines have had much better fatal accident records than other airlines in their respective regions. The excellent performances of both CSA (Czechoslovakia) and JAT (Yugoslavia) stand out compared to other Eastern European carriers. The same is true for MAS (Malaysia) in Asia; and El Al and Kuwait Airways in the Middle East. For the 1977-1989 period, there also were major carriers whose fatal accident records were significantly worse, including Avianca (Colombia), Austral (Argentina), Thai, and Air India.

Another aspect of the record of fatal accidents across airlines is that the distinction between international and domestic operations that is frequently made may be somewhat artificial. Safety statistics that rely on passenger-mile data to construct accident rates are particularly misleading when comparing international and domestic

Table 5.8 Accident and Fatality Record by Carrier, 1977-1989

Carrier	1977-1989 Departures[a] (Millions)	Fatal Accidents[a]	Fatal Adjusted Accidents[b]	Fatal Acc. per 1 Million Departures	Death Risk per 1 Million Departures
North America					
Delta	7.626	2	0.96	0.26	0.13
United	6.852	4	1.46	0.58	0.21
Eastern	6.598	1	1.00	0.15	0.15
American	6.035	2	1.32	0.33	0.22
USAir	4.774	4	1.13	0.84	0.24
TWA	3.515	1	0.03	0.28	0.01
Northwest	3.243	2	1.47	0.62	0.45
Continental	3.174	3	0.87	0.95	0.27
Air Canada	2.243	2	0.52	0.89	0.23
Southwest	1.885	0	0.00	0.00	0.00
Pan Am	1.646	4	2.52	2.43	1.53
Canadian	0.837	0	0.00	0.00	0.00
America West	0.771	0	0.00	0.00	0.00
Hawaiian	0.663	0	0.00	0.00	0.00
Alaska	0.641	0	0.00	0.00	0.00
Aloha	0.553	2	1.02	3.62	1.85
Midway	0.398	0	0.00	0.00	0.00
Quebecair	0.307	1	0.71	3.26	2.31
Air Jamaica	0.129	0	0.00	0.00	0.00
Trump Shuttle	0.006	0	0.00	0.00	0.00
Australia/ New Zealand					
Air New Zealand	0.914	0	0.00	0.00	0.00
Ansett	0.903	0	0.00	0.00	0.00
Australian	0.414	0	0.00	0.00	0.00
East-West	0.300	0	0.00	0.00	0.00
Qantas	0.248	0	0.00	0.00	0.00
Air NSW	0.190	0	0.00	0.00	0.00
Ansett WA	0.183	0	0.00	0.00	0.00
Latin America					
Varig	1.011	2	1.20	1.98	1.19
VASP	0.948	4	1.04	4.22	1.10
Mexicana	0.947	1	1.00	1.06	1.06
Aeromexico	0.933	3	2.76	3.22	2.96
Aerolineas Argentinas	0.814	0	0.00	0.00	0.00
LAV	0.645	1	1.00	1.55	1.55
Avianca	0.613	3	2.94	4.89	4.79
Transbrasil	0.547	1	0.95	1.83	1.73
Cruziero	0.540	0	0.00	0.00	0.00
Avensa	0.465	2	0.59	4.30	1.27
Austral	0.289	2	2.00	6.93	6.93

Table 5.8   (cont'd), Accident and Fatality Record by Carrier, 1977-1989

Carrier	1977-1989 Departures[a] (Millions)	Fatal Accidents[a]	Fatal Adjusted Accidents[b]	Fatal Acc. per 1 Million Departures	Death Risk per 1 Million Departures
Aeroperu	0.231	1	0.17	4.33	0.75
LAB	0.206	2	2.00	9.70	9.70
Rio-Sul	0.176	0	0.00	0.00	0.00
TAN/SAHSA	0.172	1	0.92	5.82	5.37
TAM	0.168	3	1.00	17.81	5.94
SAM	0.149	2	2.00	13.42	13.42
Faucett	0.148	0	0.00	0.00	0.00
VOTEC	0.144	1	1.00	6.94	6.94
Cubana	0.140	1	1.00	7.16	7.16
VIASA	0.127	0	0.00	0.00	0.00
Nordeste	0.127	0	0.00	0.00	0.00
TACA	0.120	0	0.00	0.00	0.00
TABA	0.116	3	2.14	25.90	18.55
LanChile	0.111	1	0.31	8.99	2.82
Ladeco	0.102	0	0.00	0.00	0.00
Pluna	0.081	0	0.00	0.00	0.00
COPA	0.064	0	0.00	0.00	0.00
CDA	0.057	0	0.00	0.00	0.00
LACSA	0.055	0	0.00	0.00	0.00
Ecuatoriana	0.054	0	0.00	0.00	0.00
Aviateca	0.038	0	0.00	0.00	0.00
Air Panama	0.037	0	0.00	0.00	0.00
Aerovias	0.034	3	3.00	88.05	88.50
LAC	0.012	0	0.00	0.00	0.00
SLM (Surinam)	0.004	1	0.88	270.27	238.11
Western Europe					
Lufthansa	2.778	1	0.05	0.36	0.02
British Airways	2.674	0	0.00	0.00	0.00
SAS	2.309	0	0.00	0.00	0.00
Iberia	2.156	2	1.53	0.93	0.71
Air France	1.996	0	0.00	0.00	0.00
Alitalia	1.289	1	0.84	0.78	0.65
Swissair	1.237	1	0.09	0.81	0.07
Air Inter	1.210	1	0.01	0.83	0.01
Linjeflyg	0.987	0	0.00	0.00	0.00
Wideroe	0.888	2	2.00	2.25	2.25
KLM	0.860	0	0.00	0.00	0.00
Olympic	0.844	1	1.00	1.19	1.19
Finnair	0.829	0	0.00	0.00	0.00
ATI	0.687	2	2.00	2.91	2.91
Sabena	0.594	0	0.00	0.00	0.00
Braathens	0.577	0	0.00	0.00	0.00
Air UK	0.475	0	0.00	0.00	0.00
British Midland	0.448	1	0.37	2.23	0.83
AerLingus	0.445	0	0.00	0.00	0.00
Aviaco	0.415	1	1.00	2.41	2.41

Table 5.8 (cont'd), Accident and Fatality Record by Carrier, 1977-1989

Carrier	1977-1989 Departures[a] (Millions)	Fatal Accidents[a]	Fatal Adjusted Accidents[b]	Fatal Acc. per 1 Million Departures	Death Risk per 1 Million Departures
Dan Air	0.382	0	0.00	0.00	0.00
Austrian	0.362	0	0.00	0.00	0.00
TAP	0.346	1	0.79	2.89	2.27
NLM	0.224	1	1.00	4.46	4.46
Crossair	0.201	0	0.00	0.00	0.00
Icelandair	0.164	0	0.00	0.00	0.00
UTA	0.153	1	1.00	6.54	6.54
Alisarda	0.125	0	0.00	0.00	0.00
SATA	0.088	0	0.00	0.00	0.00
Luxair	0.073	0	0.00	0.00	0.00
Arnarflug/ EagleAir	0.019	0	0.00	0.00	0.00
Virgin	0.013	0	0.00	0.00	0.00
Asia					
ANA	2.204	0	0.00	0.00	0.00
TOA	1.269	0	0.00	0.00	0.00
Indian	1.256	3	1.98	2.39	1.58
MAS	1.194	1	1.00	0.84	0.84
Garuda	1.126	4	2.58	3.55	2.29
JAL	1.029	3	1.55	2.92	1.50
PAL	0.736	4	2.15	5.44	2.93
KAL	0.661	4	1.48	6.05	2.24
Merpati	0.640	5	2.89	7.81	4.51
PIA	0.611	3	2.24	4.91	3.67
JapanAirSystem	0.568	0	0.00	0.00	0.00
SIA	0.410	0	0.00	0.00	0.00
Thai	0.309	3	2.78	9.71	9.00
Cathay Pacific	0.299	0	0.00	0.00	0.00
Southwest (Japan)	0.297	0	0.00	0.00	0.00
Talair	0.247	3	2.09	12.14	8.45
Air Niugini	0.236	0	0.00	0.00	0.00
Air India	0.208	3	2.17	14.45	10.46
Royal Nepal	0.205	0	0.00	0.00	0.00
Air Nippon	0.204	0	0.00	0.00	0.00
Bouraq	0.168	2	1.89	11.90	11.24
Biman	0.152	1	1.00	6.57	6.57
Vayudoot	0.075	1	1.00	13.32	13.32
Air Lanka	0.061	1	1.00	16.34	16.34
JapanAsia	0.057	0	0.00	0.00	0.00
Mandala	0.029	0	0.00	0.00	0.00
Asiana	0.019	0	0.00	0.00	0.00
Far Eastern	NA	1			
China Airlines	NA	5			
Myanmar	NA	9			
CAAC	NA	8			

Table 5.8   (cont'd), Accident and Fatality Record by Carrier, 1977-1989

Carrier	1977-1989 Departures[a] (Millions)	Fatal Accidents[a]	Fatal Adjusted Accidents[b]	Fatal Acc. per 1 Million Departures	Death Risk per 1 Million Departures
Eastern Europe					
Aeroflot	7.287	2	.82	2.88	2.45
JAT	0.549	0	0.00	0.00	0.00
LOT	0.430	3	1.05	6.98	2.45
CSA	0.391	0	0.00	0.00	0.00
Tarom	0.242	2	1.01	8.26	4.17
Malev	0.207	1	0.55	4.84	2.65
Balkan Bulgarian	NA	3			
Africa					
SAA	0.732	1	1.00	1.37	1.37
Nigeria Awys	0.372	2	1.80	5.37	4.83
Air Madagascar	0.231	0	0.00	0.00	0.00
Ethiopian	0.179	2	1.82	11.17	10.18
Air Tanzania	0.159	0	0.00	0.00	0.00
Kenya Awys	0.129	0	0.00	0.00	0.00
Air Zimbabwe	0.113	2	0.63	17.67	5.59
Zambia Airways	0.078	0	0.00	0.00	0.00
Air Zaire	0.069	0	0.00	0.00	0.00
Air Mauritius	0.063	0	0.00	0.00	0.00
Air Ivoire	0.060	0	0.00	0.00	0.00
LAM	0.057	1	0.79	17.61	13.93
Air Malta	0.057	0	0.00	0.00	0.00
Air Malawi	0.056	1	1.00	17.83	17.83
Ghanair	0.055	0	0.00	0.00	0.00
Lesotho	0.016	0	0.00	0.00	0.00
Somali	0.015	2	1.16	137.93	79.86
Air Afrique	0.013	1	0.06	76.92	4.38
Uganda	0.006	1	0.48	175.44	83.33
TAAG (Angola)	0.005	1	1.00	217.39	217.39
Air Rwanda	0.003	0	0.00	0.00	0.00
Cameroon	NA	3	2.00		
Air Mali	NA	1	1.00		
Middle East					
Saudia	1.134	2	1.02	1.76	0.90
Egyptair	0.363	0	0.00	0.00	0.00
Iran	0.357	2	2.00	5.60	5.60
Tunis Air	0.183	0	0.00	0.00	0.00
Kuwait	0.177	1	0.01	5.66	0.05
GulfAir	0.176	1	1.00	5.67	5.67
Royal Air Maroc	0.171	0	0.00	0.00	0.00
ElAl	0.141	1	0.01	7.11	0.04
Alia	0.107	1	0.70	9.36	6.59

Table 5.8 (cont'd), Accident and Fatality Record by Carrier, 1977-1989

Carrier	1977-1989 Departures[a] (Millions)	Fatal Accidents[a]	Fatal Adjusted Accidents[b]	Fatal Acc. per 1 Million Departures	Death Risk per 1 Million Departures
Cyprus	0.078	0	0.00	0.00	0.00
Syrian Arab	0.076	0	0.00	0.00	0.00
Yemen Awys	0.065	1	1.00	15.41	15.38
Iraqi	0.052	1	0.63	19.42	12.17
Alymeda (S.Yem)	NA	2			
THY (Turkey)	NA	3			

[a]Departures and accidents incorporate data from airlines acquired during the 1977-1989 period. For example, the data for Delta include departures and accidents for Western Airlines; USAir totals include the data from Piedmont.
[b]Adjusted fatal accidents are the number of fatal accidents multiplied by the percentage of passengers killed on those flights.

The worldwide average rate of fatal accidents per 1 million departures is 1.45. Any carrier with a rate of greater than 4.00 accidents per 1 million departures can be considered to have a significantly higher rate at the 95 percent confidence level. Similarly, the worldwide average death risk per 1 million departures is 0.98. Any carrier with a death risk of greater than 3.25 per 1 million departures can be considered to have a significantly higher rate at the 95 percent confidence level.

Source: Compiled from *Flight International, Aviation Week and Space Technology, Air Transport World, Interavia,* and ICAO, ADREP, various years.

operations, given the much longer average length of international flights. Several predominantly domestic airlines have maintained excellent safety records throughout the period while flying a large number of flights. Among domestic carriers averaging more than 200 daily flights, Mexicana, Linjeflyg (Sweden), Air Inter (France), and TOA (Japan) all achieved excellent accident records. In general, there seems to be a close correspondence between the safety performance of a country's international and domestic operations. The exceptions to this correspondence are in the larger South American countries, where domestic operations experienced much poorer accident records. Also, there were few differences between the domestic and international safety records of those airlines operating both types of service.

THE SAFETY RECORD OF NONSCHEDULED (CHARTER) AIRLINES

Given the important role played by charter airlines in much of the world, an examination of safety rates must not be limited to scheduled air service. However, the total number of departures is small and data reporting is erratic for the vast majority of charter operators, so construction of individual charter carrier accident rates does not provide meaningful information.

Table 5.9 presents ICAO reported data for accidents, fatalities, and aircraft losses for nonscheduled air service from 1977 to 1986. Table 5.9 is divided into two parts: the first section covers airplanes over 27,000 kilograms gross weight, which are basically those jet

Table 5.9 Accidents and Fatalities, Nonscheduled Airline Service, 1977-1986

Year	Number of Accidents Fatal	Nonfatal	Number of Fatalities	Number of Aircraft Destroyed
	Airplanes over 27,000 kg (Jet Aircraft)			
1977	11	9	693	12
1978	0	6	0	1
1979	3	8	268	3
1980	2	7	153	5
1981	3	5	196	3
1982	2	4	55	2
1983	1	3	7	1
1984	4	7	83	6
1985	5	6	395	5
1986	1	5	3	2
Total	32	60	1,853	40
	Airplanes between 2,250-27,000 kg (Turboprop Aircraft)			
1977	31	98	175	38
1978	13	52	77	11
1979	17	73	86	21
1980	18	62	60	17
1981	15	68	95	16
1982	25	69	79	27
1983	24	77	76	29
1984	31	83	142	40
1985	29	79	82	37
1986	25	77	122	34
Total	228	738	994	270

Source: ICAO, *ADREP Annual Statistics.*

aircraft that are also commonly used by scheduled airlines. The second part of Table 5.9 shows similar data for aircraft between 2,250 kilograms and 27,000 kilograms gross weight, a category that includes virtually all types of turboprop aircraft used in passenger service, but also includes business aircraft and the general aviation fleet. Thus, the numbers reported in the bottom of the table may overstate slightly the number of accidents by charter operators.

As was done for scheduled service, a more current and comprehensive listing of nonscheduled fatal accidents was constructed from *Flight International* data (Table 5.10) Over the entire period, the probability of a fatal accident by a jet charter operator was about 8 in 1 million; the death risk was just over 6 in 1 million. However, the safety performance improved significantly in the 1983-1989 period compared to the 1977-1982 period. Thus, while nonscheduled airlines had a fatal accident record about 3.4

Table 5.10   Nonscheduled Safety Record, 1977-1989

Year	Number of Fatal Accidents	Number of Fatalities	Fatal Accidents per 1 Million Departures	Death Risk per 1 Million Departures
1977	13	779	25.40	15.36
1978	6	244	10.63	8.41
1979	3	285	5.74	4.12
1980	6	203	12.07	9.11
1981	4	278	7.52	6.64
1982	3	109	7.84	3.19
1983	3	45	6.17	6.17
1984	1	5	1.91	1.91
1985	5	484	8.35	7.23
1986	1	87	1.61	1.61
1987	1	183	1.71	1.71
1988	4	84	6.97	5.12
1989	7	418	11.11	10.03
1977-1989	57	3204	8.11	6.21
1977-1982	35	1898	11.63	7.99
1983-1989	22	1306	5.48[a]	4.87

[a]The 1983-1989 rate is lower than the 1977-1982 rate at the 95 percent confidence level.

Source: Compiled from *Flight International, Aviation Week and Space Technology, Air Transport World, Interavia,* and ICAO, ADREP, various years.

times worse and a death risk about 3.9 times worse than did scheduled carriers, their relative performance improved substantially in the past five years. For the 1983-1989 period, the charter airline fatal accident rate was about twice that of scheduled airlines, and death risk was about 2.7 times worse than scheduled service, both of which represent improvements in absolute terms as well as relative to scheduled service.

The high load factors on charter operations are reflected in the large number of fatalities per accident. As mentioned previously, the world's worst air disaster involved the on-ground high speed collision of KLM and Pan Am charter flight at Tenerife in 1977. In fact, six of the fifteen worst fatal accidents between 1977 and 1989 involved charter airlines. However, Spantax was the only charter operator to be involved in more than one fatal accident over the period. There is no apparent geographic pattern in the charter accidents.

THE CAUSES OF INTERNATIONAL FATAL ACCIDENTS

Information from ICAO and from additional public sources can be used to gain some insight into the causes of world airline accidents. Before presenting the results, several data limitations should be mentioned. First, as mentioned, the ICAO ADREP data is the only comprehensive, official set of accident records worldwide. There is a significant time lag before the records are compiled, limiting use of this resource to accidents occurring through 1986. Second, the amount of information reported to ICAO from individual countries or airlines varies markedly. Many of the accident reports published in the ICAO accident summaries are missing objective information on weather conditions and similar items. Third, the published summary descriptions frequently are insufficient to establish an accident event sequence so essential in determining the sequence-initiating cause. Finally, the definitions and standards used in accident determinations vary across countries and across organizations which collect safety data. Thus, while the analysis based on ICAO information is useful, it is not directly comparable to the U.S. and Canadian accident analyses presented in prior chapters.

ICAO Data on International Accidents, 1977-1986

The ICAO ADREP system provides summary information on aviation accidents from reporting member countries. Table 5.11

presents the distribution of accidents by phase of operation between 1977 and 1986. Three fourths of all accidents occur during takeoff and climb or during approach and landing. The frequency of en route accidents is higher worldwide than it is in the United States. This remains true even if terrorist-related accidents are excluded.

Table 5.12 shows the distribution of principal events that led to accidents as reported by ICAO. As was discussed in detail in Chapter 2, a given accident may have involved more than one occurrence or factor. The information in Table 5.12 presents all 1977-1986 accidents in which a specific event was deemed by ICAO to be the primary cause of the accident. The first important feature of Table 5.12 is that only 74 percent of all accidents were classified by ICAO. The distribution of events is quite broad. Only five categories—collision with terrain; loss of control; engine failure; collapse of landing gear; and collision with another object— comprised more than 10 percent of the total accidents that were classified.

Table 5.12 provides a profile of the types of events that precipitated airline accidents, but it fails to provide much information about why these events occurred—the real cause of the accident. Without this information, accident reports can be difficult to interpret. For example, the collapse of landing gear may be due to a mechanical problem, the pilot's failure to lower the gear in time, or a particularly hard landing on the runway. Even an event like engine failure is subject to some degree of ambiguity. For example, an engine that experiences broken turbine

Table 5.11 Accidents by Phase of Operation as Reported by ICAO, 1977-1986

	Number	Percentage of Total
Taxi	193	4.6
En Route	832	20.0
Takeoff/Climb	1392	33.4
Approach/Landing	1640	39.4
Standing	109	2.6
Total	4166	100.0

Source: Compiled from ICAO, ADREP.

Table 5.12 Typology of Accidents by Primary Event,[a] ICAO
Classification, 1977-1986

Engine Failure	334
Gear Retracted/	355
Collapsed	
Airframe Failure	45
Loss of Control	438
Hard Landing	77
Undershoot	114
Overshoot	179
Collision-Object	299
Collision-Birds	8
Collision-Terrain	384
Damage to Aircraft in flight	33
Damage to Aircraft on ground	27
Injuries to Persons on ground	76
Fire/Explosion	119
Other	86
TOTAL	2574
Total Accidents in ICAO ADREP System	3478

[a](Primary event found in 2574/3478 = 74% of accidents)

Source: ICAO, ADREP, various years.

blades presents a different situation than an engine that fails because of fuel mismanagement.

To remedy this situation (to a limited extent), ICAO reports accident data according to principal cause. These data are presented in Table 5.13 for 1977-1982 and for 1983-1986. The table illustrates a serious problem with ICAO-reported accident analysis. First, in the 1977-1982 period only 69.5 percent of all accidents were classified into the four categories shown. But from 1983 to 1986, almost 95 percent of accident causes fell into one of the four categories. The result was to increase pilot error as the cause from 41 percent to 59 percent, and to double the percentage of accidents

Table 5.13 Principal Accident Causes as Reported by ICAO, 1977-1982 and 1983-1986

	1977-1982		1983-1986	
Pilot Error	832	(40.9)[a]	590	(58.8)
Aircraft or Engine	176	(8.6)	160	(16.0)
Airport	66	(3.3)	54	(5.4)
Weather	339	(16.7)	147	(14.7)

[a]Percentages are shown in parentheses. They are shown as percentages of total accidents, not of the numbers shown here. The four causal factors shown here represent 69.5% of accidents in 1977-1982 and 94.9% of accidents in 1983-1985.

Source: ICAO, *ADREP*, various years.

related to equipment and engine failures. Unfortunately, there is no way to determine whether this reported increase was due to actual increases in pilot error and equipment failure or due to an increased willingness on the part of ICAO to classify accidents according to these groups.

Accident Analysis Based on Other Sources

ICAO data represent the most comprehensive official information on worldwide airline accidents. However, the problem of classification and the lack of more recent ICAO accident data make it worthwhile to construct accident analysis data similar to that presented earlier for the United States and Canada. The basic data come from *Flight International*'s aviation safety accident reports for each year. The classification of accident causes attempts to parallel as closely as possible the methods used for U.S. and Canadian carriers in Chapters 2, 3, and 4. However, a number of limitations should be mentioned.

First, unlike analyses based on U.S. or ICAO data, this analysis is limited to fatal accidents. The data presented in *Flight International* aggregate nonfatal accidents and incidents, so that it is difficult to identify the severity of an event. Second, information on fatal accidents that occurred between 1977 and 1986 reflects both *Flight International* and ICAO reports. Since ICAO data were unavailable for the years beyond 1986, causal factors were drawn from information collected on each accident from public sources, including *Flight International, Air Transport World, Aviation Week and Space Technology, Interavia,* and other industry publications.

While the resulting data are unofficial and the information is unavailable in consistent form, they represent more up-to-date information and, thus, help provide a preliminary assessment.

In reporting accident causes on a worldwide basis, it is essential to incorporate not only the different mix of causes, but also to account for the differential regional rates at which accidents occur. Put another way, one wants to know not just how likely is an accident in the North America due to pilot error, but rather how much more likely is a fatal accident due to pilot error in Africa than in North America. To do this, each accident was classified into one of twelve primary causes. The total fatal accident rates by region then were broken down by cause to construct accident rates by primary cause. To illustrate, the overall North American fatal accident rate per 1,000,000 departures for 1977-1989 was 0.88, which can be decomposed into primary cause categories. The fatal accident rate in North America due to engine failure was 0.06 per 1,000,000 departures; this is equivalent to saying that 0.06/0.88 = 0.07 or 7 percent of the fatal accidents in North America were due to engine failure.

The results are shown in Table 5.14. The regional variations in accident rates by primary cause are of greatest interest. Latin America's accident rate due to engine failure of 0.66 is eleven times greater than that of North America. The data show much higher accident rates due to engine failures in Eastern Europe and Africa as well. The rate of engine failure was particularly high on Soviet-built aircraft. Terrorist activity was involved in 22 percent of African fatal accidents and 29 percent of all fatal accidents in the Middle East during the period. The rate of pilot error accidents is relatively high in Latin America, Asia, and Africa.

Weather is a much more frequent factor in accidents in the developing world than in North America or Western Europe. Part of this is due to difficult climates in parts of South America, Asia, and Africa. However, the striking difference between developed and developing regions suggests that the frequency of weather-related accidents might be substantially reduced if more detailed, timely weather information was available to pilots in less developed countries. Given the technological advances in weather forecasting and reporting, such information might help pilots avoid difficult weather situations in many regions. Also, the frequent lack of, or inadequacy of, landing aids in less developed regions make it more difficult to cope with weather-related factors.

In general, the widely disparate accident rates across regions cannot be attributed predominantly to one or two factors or to a particularly difficult operating environment. For example, in

Table 5.14   Fatal Accident Rates[a] by Primary Accident Cause, By
Geographic Region, 1977 - 1989

Primary Cause	US/ Canada	Latin Amer.	West. Europe	East. Europe	Asia	Africa	Middle East
Engine Failure	.06	.66	.09	1.03	.23	2.25	.00
Equipment Failure	.17	.66	.05	.45	.47	1.46	.38
Weather	.10	1.45	.32	.45	1.30	.80	1.59
Pilot Error	.32	2.11	.41	.78	1.54	2.52	.38
Air Traffic Control	.02	.12	.00	.00	.09	.00	.00
Ground Crew	.02	.12	.00	.12	.00	.00	.00
General Aviation	.04	.00	.00	.12	.00	.53	.00
Terrorism	.00	.12	.05	.25	.42	2.92	1.15
Icing	.04	.00	.09	.25	.00	.00	.00
Terrain	.04	.30	.07	.25	.14	1.86	1.59
Fire	.00	.00	.00	.00	.00	.53	.00
Other	.07	.48	.07	.41	.47	.40	.38
Total Accident Rate	.88	6.04	1.15	4.11	4.66	13.25	5.47
Number of Fatal Accidents	63	64	30	33	63	31	17

[a]Fatal accidents per 1 million aircraft departures.

Source: Compiled from *Flight International, Aviation Week and Space Technology, Air Transport World, Interavia,* and ICAO, ADREP (various years). Accidents are classified by location, not by nationality of airlines involved. "Other" category includes animal strikes and accidents not otherwise classified or for which insufficient data were available to determine primary cause. Zero values indicate that this factor was not determined to be a primary cause for any of the accidents in that region.

addition to the dramatically higher rate of accidents caused by terrorism, Africa experienced accident rates due to engine failure that were 37 times worse than that for North America, equipment failure rates 8.6 times worse, weather-related accident rates 8 times worse, and pilot error rates 8 times worse. A similar pattern of high accident rates across a wide range of causes is found in Latin America. The regional variation in aggregate rates typically reflects across-the-board problems rather than differences in a single type of accident. Improvements in airline safety in the developing world would seem to require improvements in aircraft maintenance, technology, and human factors.

While examining the accident experience of carriers both in the United States and throughout the world provides important insights into aviation safety, analyses based only on accidents are quite limited. An accident is clear evidence that some element of safety was inadequate on that flight, but waiting until safety problems become apparent in accident data is a slow and costly way to detect emerging safety issues. Accidents are rare events even among the riskiest segments of the industry and in developing countries. By the time a safety problem can be detected in the accident experience, it is likely that many people will have been killed and injured. Thus, people have increasingly turned their attention to finding nonaccident safety indicators that would be more sensitive to underlying changes in the safety of the system and might point to emerging problems before accidents occurred. These nonaccident indicators are the topic of the next chapter.

II

EMERGING SAFETY ISSUES

Chapter 6

The Margin of Safety

As discussed in Chapter 2, the safety record of the U.S. passenger airline industry, as measured by both aircraft accident rates and passenger fatality rates, has continued to improve throughout the post-deregulation period. Even the PATCO strike in 1981, although it put considerable pressure on the air traffic control system, did not appear to have had an adverse impact on safety.[1] Moreover, the safety improvement extends across all segments of the jet carrier industry as well as individual carriers.[2]

Despite this improvement, some still fear that deterioration in safety is an inevitable consequence of economic deregulation.[3] One widespread concern has been articulated by John Lauber, a member of the NTSB, "An accident is clear evidence that safety is lacking, but, by itself, the absence of an accident does not demonstrate that safety has been achieved. What is needed is a set of 'leading safety indicators' along the lines of the 'leading economic indicators,' and these should be used to examine further the effects of airline deregulation."[4]

In principle, leading safety indicators could allow safety problems to be identified and corrected as they emerge without

---

[1]William A. Cunningham and Grant M. Davis, "A Preliminary Analysis of the Impact of the PATCO Strike on Airline Safety," *Journal of the Transportation Research Forum* 28 (1) (1987): 21-24.

[2]Richard Golaszewski and Earl Bomberger, "Measuring Differential Safety Performance Among Air Carriers," *Transportation Research Forum Proceedings* 27 (1) (1986): 12-21.

[3]John Nance, "Economic Deregulation's Uninteneded but Inevitable Impact on Airline Safety," in Leon Moses and Ian Savage, *Transportation Safety in an Age of Deregulation*, (New York: Oxford University Press, 1989), pp. 186-205.

[4]*Ibid*, p. 203.

having to wait for a tragic accident to point to weaknesses in the system. The analogy with leading economic indicators, however, is deceptive and the search for leading nonaccident safety indicators is likely to be difficult. Even a simple relationship between the rate of nonaccident events and the rate of accidents has yet to be established clearly, which does not even begin to establish a set of indicators that can act as a precursor to a change in the rate of accidents.

Aviation safety relies on both reliability and redundancy. Some parts of the system have been made more reliable through better design and construction and through better inspection techniques that allow detection of prospective problems prior to failure. Other parts of the aviation system are designed to tolerate some failure—electrical, mechanical, or human—in aircraft operations or air traffic control without a resulting accident. Such redundancy can provide a "margin of safety" that allows failure of an individual component without disastrous consequences. It is a testimony to the success of this philosophy that airline accidents have become rare events that are usually the result of several concurrent failures.

The term *margin of safety* can create confusion, however, because it has different meanings to different people. As used by some, it refers to a loosely defined "extra cushion" of safety that is not expected to be needed, but might be.[5] In this usage, the greater the margin of safety, the better. Among structural engineers, however, margin of safety has a more precise definition: {(Capability -Requirement)/Requirement}. For example, a structural component with a margin of safety of 0.1 has a 10 percent greater strength than needed. A perfect design would have a zero margin of safety, meaning that it was strong enough for its needs without any extra strength, which translates into extra weight and higher cost. Of course, for a zero margin of safety to be perfect design, the requirement would have to be known with certainty. Such exact knowledge of the requirements is not common in aviation; thus, margin of safety, as used in this context, refers to the less exact definition—extra cushion.

Reliance on redundancy complicates the assessment of changes in safety. Accidents and fatalities are the best long-run indicators of aviation safety—after all, preventing fatal accidents is the ultimate goal—but accident data are poorly suited for quick detection of changes in the underlying safety of the system. For example, for many functions in an aircraft, additional safety is

[5]Aviation Safety Commission, *Volume I: Final Report and Recommendations* (Washington, D.C.: Government Printing Office, April 1988).

provided by having a backup system for those rare occurrences when the primary system fails. An increase in the frequency of failure in the primary system would result in more frequent reliance upon backup systems. Backup systems can also fail; so, eventually, increased use of backup systems could lead to more accidents. Thus, increased primary system failure would be a clear reduction in the underlying safety of the system even though, in the overwhelming majority of primary system failures, there would be no accident.

How can this reduction in safety be detected with accident data? Over the long run, the higher primary system failure rate eventually would result in more accidents. How many accidents are necessary before a clear change in the underlying safety of the system can be identified? While a precise answer is in the murky realm of statistics, it would generally take a great deal of time, and quite a few accidents, to detect such a change with confidence. No one is comfortable with having to wait for accidents to identify safety problems. More sensitive measures of changes in the underlying safety of the aviation system are needed—measures that can detect changes in the margin of safety.

THE MARGIN OF SAFETY

Conceptually, the margin of safety can be thought of either as a threshold or as a continuum. The threshold approach is closest to the structural engineer's definition and can be illustrated with the analogy of a bridge. In building a bridge, the design engineer will try to avoid structural failure by designing for the greatest load that will ever be needed. The engineer may incorporate extra strength as a margin of safety for the bridge to allow for unanticipated loads, substandard materials, slight errors in construction, or deterioration of the materials over time. An overly cautious design engineer may build a margin of safety into the bridge that is so great that a reduction in the unneeded strength might have been possible without increasing the risk of using the bridge. In practice, a bridge that is five times as strong as necessary may be no safer than one that is only four times as strong as necessary. At some point, however, the margin of safety could become so thin as to cause concern. Any structure built to accommodate only a 1 percent greater load than the maximum anticipated may rely too heavily on the designer's ability to anticipate the loads to which the structure will be subjected and on the builder's ability to execute the design.

For a bridge, the margin of safety can be thought of as the extra strength that the designer never expects to need but puts in nonetheless. For aviation, the margin of safety can be thought of as the extra cushion that should never be needed if everything works as anticipated. This extra cushion can take many forms, including aircraft components built to greater strengths than are expected to be required or aircraft separation standards in the air traffic control system that are far greater than expected to be necessary to keep aircraft from colliding.

An alternative concept of a margin of safety is to think of safety as a continuum where any increase in the margin of safety reduces the probability of an accident. With the continuum approach there are two ways to improve safety of a component of the aviation system. One way is to make the component more reliable and less likely to fail. Another way is to take the redundancy approach and provide a backup system to take over if the primary system fails. In practice, aviation safety has been improved both by enhancing the reliability of individual components and by providing redundancy in the form of backup systems.

The fundamental difference between the two approaches is that with the threshold concept some reduction in the margin of safety may be possible without increasing the risk of accident, whereas with the continuum concept any reduction in the margin of safety increases the risk of accident. Redundant systems can be thought of as an outgrowth of the continuum concept. The greater the number of backup systems, the smaller the probability of total failure. A reduction in the number of backup systems increases the risk of accident, although the increase in risk may be extremely small.

While both the threshold and the continuum approach to the margin of safety are useful conceptually, neither lends itself to precise definition or measurement. The margin of safety has many dimensions, some of which are best thought of as a continuum while others are best thought of as a threshold. Any single index of the margin of safety would have to combine both concepts.

USING INCIDENT DATA

An accident provides indisputable, after-the-fact evidence that some element of safety for that particular flight was inadequate. As seen earlier, examining airline accidents can provide considerable insight into persistent safety problems in various segments of the industry. However, examining accidents may not be the best way to detect emerging safety problems. Instead, changes in the frequency of safety-related problems (incidents) may provide more sensitive measures of changing probabilities of aviation accidents. The value of incident data analysis hinges, first, on a correlation between incidents and accidents and, second, on the premise that careful tracking of changes in incidents may point to problems before they become apparent in accident data.

Incidents vary widely in the risk posed to passengers. Events that remain incidents may differ little from those that develop into serious accidents. The line between an event that has the potential to result in property damage, injury, or death, and one that poses little or no risk is often hard to draw. For example, most would agree that a near midair collision that leaves less than 100 feet separation between aircraft is a serious incident. However, few would argue that airplanes and lives are jeopardized by loss of aircraft separation from five miles to four miles. At what point does a loss of separation begin to pose a risk?

Unlike accident data, which are compiled from the investigations of the NTSB and similar organizations in other countries, incident data have been developed by various groups in the aviation community to assess specific questions of interest to them. These specialized data may be difficult to apply to other, more broadly defined, questions. For example, airline operators, aircraft manufacturers, and engine manufacturers may all track incidents associated with a specific type of engine in order to evaluate its performance and assess the need for special maintenance programs. Each group, however, may have its own approach to data collection and storage so that the data sets are not entirely compatible with one another nor can they be easily linked together. Even the various incident databases maintained by the FAA were each developed by different parts of the agency with specific problems in mind.

Examples of incident databases include, but are not limited to, the FAA's accident incident data system, aviation standards service difficulty data system, near midair collision (NMAC) database, operational error database, pilot deviation database, air operator data system, air traffic activity database, NASA's Aviation Safety Reporting System, the NTSB's aviation accident data system, and Boeing's safety data system. While these databases are difficult and in some cases virtually impossible to combine into a consistent, integrated source of information on hazardous incidents, each can provide some insight into aviation safety, as long as the limitations of the particular data are understood.

MIDAIR COLLISIONS

Some of the most intense concern about aviation safety, particularly in the media, has been with midair collisions. Three types of incidents are often believed to be associated with the risk of midair collisions: *air traffic control operational errors*, *pilot deviations*, and *near midair collisions*.

Operational Errors

An overriding goal of the air traffic control system is to keep aircraft under its control separated from other aircraft and from obstructions. An *operational error* is " ... an occurrence attributable to an element of the air traffic control system which results in less than the applicable separation minima between two or more aircraft, or between an aircraft and terrain or obstacles and obstructions ... [o]bstacles include: vehicles/equipment/personnel on runways."[6]

Table 6.1 shows that total reported operational errors have risen from 491 in 1976 to 916 in 1989. From 1983 to 1984 errors more than doubled. They then decreased slightly in 1985 and 1986, remained essentially the same in 1987, and fell again in 1988 and 1989. The large increase in errors in 1984 can be attributed, to a large extent, to implementation of the operational error detection program (OEDP). The OEDP, called the "snitch patch" by controllers, is a computer program that automatically records violations of en route separation standards at ARTCCs, removing any discretion in filing operational error reports. Prior to 1984, reports of operational errors were filed on a voluntary basis; fear of disciplinary action may have reduced reported errors during those years. Operational error reporting has not been computerized at terminal facilities and is still based on reports filed by controllers.

The sharp increase in reported operational errors highlights a problem with most incident data. If any discretion is involved in filing reports, sensitivity and awareness of a problem or issue may increase the propensity to report. On the other hand, fear of repercussions may decrease the propensity to report. Thus, distinguishing between a change in the underlying problem and a change in the propensity to report or, in this case, the method of reporting, can be almost impossible.

[6]U.S. Department of Transportation, Federal Aviation Administration, Office of Aviation Safety, *National Aviation System Airspace Incidents, Summary Fact Sheet*, mimeographed, January 20, 1988.

Table 6.1   Operational Errors versus Total Operations[a], 1976-1989

Year	Total Errors	Total Instrument[a] Operations	Total Airport Tower	Overall error rate (per 100,000 air traffic operations)
1976	491	53,567,508	63,974,621	0.42
1977	507	57,492,041	66,724,291	0.41
1978	571	61,512,108	67,173,434	0.44
1979	612	66,134,739	69,039,372	0.45
1980	586	68,237,921	66,195,066	0.44
1981	457	66,752,601	61,570,457	0.36
1982	353	59,517,829	50,634,988	0.32
1983	723	63,400,599	53,320,931	0.62
1984	1,888	68,942,532	56,958,937	1.50
1985	1,402	71,827,106	58,020,808	1.08
1986	1,202	75,939,397	60,431,306	0.88
1987	1,199	80,075,146	61,868,531	0.84
1988	1,037	81,428,568	62,527,547	0.72
1989	916	82,051,714	62,684,786	0.63

[a]Includes total instrument operations (ARTCC and Approach Control) and total airport tower operations.

Source: U.S. Department of Transportation, FAA, Office of the Associate Administrator for Aviation Safety, *Aviation Safety Statistics: Annual Summary Calendar Year 1989*, mimeographed, May 15, 1990.

Table 6.2 indicates that the en route share of total operational errors increased dramatically in 1983 and 1984, apparently in large part due to both the increased attention being paid to these errors and to the removal of the discretion involved in reporting. When the snitch patch was introduced, controllers had difficulty making distinctions between aircraft separated by slightly more than the required five miles and those separated by slightly less than five miles. Faced with a sharp increase in operational errors reported by the snitch patch, controllers responded by increasing separation well beyond the five-mile range. Beginning in 1986, computer software used by enroute controllers was refined so

Table 6.2 Operational Errors by Year[a]

A. Total Errors by Category

Year	Terminal		Enroute	(ARTCC)	Flight Service Station (FSS)		Total
1980	356	(60.8)	230	(39.2)	0		586
1981	289	(63.2)	168	(14.8)	0		457
1982	188	(53.3)	164	(46.5)	1	(0.2)	353
1983	292	(40.4)	429	(59.3)	2	(0.3)	723
1984	388	(20.6)	1497	(79.3)	3	(0.1)	1888
1985	409	(29.1)	992	(70.7)	3	(0.2)	1404
1986	395	(32.9)	807	(67.1)	0		1202
1987	398	(33.2)	800	(66.7)	1	(0.1)	1199
1988	372	(35.7)	664	(64.1)	2	(0.2)	1037
1989	346	(37.8)	568	(62.0)	2	(0.2)	916

B. ARTCC Errors by Level of Severity[b]

Year	Total Errors	Major		Moderate		Minor		Other	
1985[c]	992	3	(0.3)	139	(14.0)	847	(85.4)	3	(0.3)
1986[c]	808	9	(1.1)	136	(16.8)	646	(80.0)	17	(2.1)
1987	820	7	(0.9)	151	(18.4)	645	(78.7)	17	(2.1)

[a]Percentage of total in parentheses.
[b]Data not yet available to categorize the severity of the 1037 operational errors which occurred in 1988 or the 916 in 1989.
[c] To highlight one of the data problems, the data reported in the *Air Traffic Operational Error Analysis* do not exactly match the data reported in the *National Aviation System Airspace Incidents* summary.

Source: U.S. Department of Transportation, FAA, Office of Air Traffic Evaluations and Analysis, *Air Traffic Operational Error Analysis, Fiscal Year 1986*; Office of Aviation Safety, *National Aviation System Airspace Incidents, 1989 Summary Fact Sheet*, mimeographed, May 15, 1990; and data derived from computer files provided by the Office of Aviation Safety; *Aviation Safety Statistics: Annual Summary, Calendar Year 1988*, mimeographed, May 15, 1990.

that a five-mile separation "halo" around each aircraft could be displayed on the screens. Aided by this new computer software, controllers were able to maintain separation standards more precisely.

Table 6.2 also shows that the lion's share of operational errors and most of the variability are due to en route (ARTCC) errors. While declining as a percentage of total errors, the number of terminal area errors mirrored the changes in air traffic in the early 1980s and has remained relatively constant since 1984. The persistence of these terminal area errors caused the FAA to form an Operational Error Task Force in 1987. The task force made 113 recommendations, 93 of which have been implemented. Primary emphasis is on improving controller decision making and improving communications between pilots and controllers, especially in terminal areas.

En route errors are categorized by their level of severity (major, moderate, minor, and other) based on a system that assigns points for the seriousness of the violation of horizontal and vertical separation standards. To be classified as a major en route operational error, the sum of the horizontal and vertical classification must equal twenty points—the maximum number of points. Thus, for a major error, there must be both horizontal separation of less than one half mile (worth ten points) and less than 500 feet vertical separation (worth ten points).

A moderate error carries a value of fourteen to nineteen points. This type of error falls in the following ranges:

- Horizontal separation of less than one half mile (ten points) and vertical separation from 500 feet up to 600 feet (nine points) to vertical separation from 800 feet up to 900 feet (four points).

- Vertical separation of less than 500 feet (ten points) and horizontal separation of one half mile to less than one mile (eight points) to horizontal separation of two and one half miles to less than three miles (four points).

A minor operational error carries a value of thirteen points or less and falls in the following ranges:

- Horizontal separation of one mile to less than one and one half miles (seven points) and vertical separation from 700 feet up to 800 feet (six points) to vertical separation from 900 feet up to 1000 feet (two points).

- Vertical separation of 700 feet up to 800 feet (six points) and horizontal separation of one and one half miles to less than two miles (six points) to horizontal separation of four miles to less than five miles (one point).

Table 6.2 suggests that very few ARTCC operational errors (1.1 percent or less) were classified as major errors between 1985 and 1987. Even major and moderate errors combined constituted less than twenty percent of en route operational errors. These data, coupled with conversations with controllers, suggest the initial increase in reports following the snitch patch were primarily for minor errors, although the lack of pre-1985 data makes it impossible to tell for sure. In addition to changes in reporting, however, increased operations may well have had an impact on operational errors. As the airways and airspace around major airports become more congested, greater pressure is placed on controllers and more errors may result.

Pilot Deviations

Pilot deviations refer to . . . "[t]he actions of a pilot that result in the violation of a Federal Aviation Regulation or a North American Aerospace Defense Command (NORAD) Air Defense Identification Zone (ADIZ) tolerance."[7] Pilot deviation reports are filed by air traffic control, but data are only available since 1985.

As can be seen in Table 6.3, pilot deviations increased dramatically between 1985 and 1987, before declining 20 percent in 1988 and 16 percent in 1989. The table also indicates that at least through 1987 general aviation operators are responsible for a growing number and share of pilot deviations, accounting for more than 53 percent of total deviations during the period.

The bottom portion of Table 6.3 shows the distribution of pilot deviations among type of deviation in 1987 through 1989. As can be seen, the share of airspace violations has declined as the shares of ATC clearance and surface violations have grown. The decline in the number of deviations from losing standard separation was due in part to the role of both "snitch patch" and the improved controller software (mentioned earlier). However, the FAA acknowledges several limitations associated with the data base.

---

[7]U.S. Department of Transportation, Federal Aviation Administration, Office of Aviation Safety, *National Aviation System Airspace Incidents, 1987 Summary Fact Sheet*, mimeographed, January 20, 1988.

Table 6.3 Pilot Deviation Reports

		A. Categories			
	Total Pilot Deviations	Loss of Standard Separation	General Aviation	Airspace Violated	NMAC Report Filed
1985	1783	770	1010	453	32
1986	2566	1108	1354	1425	38
1987	3657	583	2159	2086	32
1988	2957	NA	NA	NA	NA
1989	2476	NA	NA	NA	NA

	B. Percentage Distribution of Deviations			
	Airspace Violation (%)	ATC Clearance (%)	Surface Violation (%)	Other (%)
1987	52	25	17	7
1988	48	26	19	7
1989	41	29	23	8

The sum of the category columns exceeds the total number of deviations, since some deviations involve more than one factor.

Source: U. S. Department of Transportation, FAA, Office of Aviation Safety, Safety Analysis Division, *Selected Statistics Concerning Reported Pilot Deviations (1985-1986)*, mimeographed, October 1987; data derived from computer files provided by the Office of Aviation Safety; *Aviation Safety Statistics: Annual Calendar Year 1989*, mimeographed, May 15, 1990.

"Automatic reporting of altitude errors in the en route environment through the Air Traffic Control (ATC) system, stepped up enforcement policies against Terminal Control Area (TCA) violators, and an overall awareness on the part of controllers concerning pilot deviation incidents has greatly affected the volume of reports received. . . ."[8] Part of the increase may represent increased risk

[8]U.S. Department of Transportation, Federal Aviation Administration, Office of Aviation Safety, Safety Analysis Division, *Report of the Pilot Deviation Task Force*, Interim Report, September, 1987. A TCA violator is most commonly an aircraft which enters the airspace surrounding an airport without required communications equipment—for example, general aviation aircraft without Mode C transponders. These planes are difficult to track on controller radar screens.

from more pilot deviations, but part may be due to more stringent reporting practices as a result of the automated reporting systems and increased awareness of pilot deviations in the aftermath of the midair collision over Cerritos, California, in August 1986.

Midair Collisions and Near Midair Collisions

Table 6.4 lists midair collisions by year from 1968 to 1989. During that time there were 608 midair collisions in the United States, an average of just under twenty-eight per year. The number of midair collisions has changed little, especially following deregulation. Of these accidents, approximately 85 percent involved two general aviation aircraft. Perhaps the most surprising feature of Table 6.4 is that 43 percent of midair collisions did not involve fatalities. However, two of the fatal accidents did involve jet carriers and substantial loss of life.

Table 6.4 Midair Collisions by Year, 1968-1989

Year	Total	Fatal	Fatalities
1968	37	23	69
1969	28	12	122
1970	37	21	55
1971	32	20	95 (1)[a]
1972	25	13	41
1973	24	12	29
1974	34	19	48
1975	29	13	47
1976	31	24	64
1977	34	17	41
1978	35	23	189 (7)[a]
1979	26	14	34
1980	25	20	58
1981	30	13	47
1982	29	18	59
1983	12	7	22
1984	25	14	47
1985	25	14	36
1986	29	17	136 (15)[a]
1987	25	13	42
1988	19	9	14
1989	17	11	36

[a]On ground fatalities in parentheses.

Source: U.S. Department of Transportation, FAA, Office of the Associate Administrator for Aviation Safety, *Aviation Safety Statistics: Annual Summary Calendar Year 1989,* mimeographed, May 15, 1990.

In 1978, a Pacific Southwest Airlines B-727 collided with a four-seat Cessna 172 in the immediate vicinity of San Diego's Lindbergh Field. Both aircraft had been receiving radar traffic advisories from controllers. Prior to the accident, however, the PSA jet had reported the Cessna to be in sight and consequently, under standard air traffic control practices, had accepted responsibility for separation from the Cessna. The collision occurred at a time when the PSA flight crew had lost visual contact with the Cessna but had not yet requested controllers to resume their radar-based traffic separation responsibility. In 1986, an Aeromexico DC-9 airliner collided with a four-seat Piper Archer. The two aircraft collided inside the Los Angeles TCA, airspace that is reserved for aircraft that have been identified on radar and cleared to proceed by air traffic controllers. The Piper had not received clearance to enter the TCA. Such accidents, coupled with the dramatic post-deregulation growth in air carrier traffic, have heightened concerns about midair collisions and those concerns have focused on reports of near midair collisions collected by the FAA and NASA-Ames.

A *near midair collision* is defined as " . . . an incident associated with the operation of an aircraft in which a possibility of collision occurs as a result of proximity of less than 500 feet to another aircraft, or an official report is received from an air crew member stating that a collision hazard existed between two or more aircraft."[9] The first part of the definition—two aircraft with less than 500 feet separation between them—provides a standard for when a near midair collision incident has occurred, but judging distance under near midair collision circumstances clearly involves some subjectivity. The pilots of both aircraft are almost certainly startled to see another aircraft that close; if they had seen one another earlier, separation would not have been lost. Moreover, when the aircraft are that close, the pilots' principal concern is evasive action, not distance estimation.

The second part of the definition—the existence of a collision hazard—adds even more subjectivity. Near midair collision reports are filed by pilots. The perception of risk in a near midair collision and the propensity to report may vary among pilots and also vary over time. For example, if more attention is paid to the issue in the media, pilots may be more inclined to report such incidents. There are two major sources of near midair collision data—the FAA's Office of Aviation Safety database and NASA's

[9]U.S. Department of Transportation, Federal Aviation Administration, Office of Aviation Safety, *National Aviation System Airspace Incidents, 1987 Summary Fact Sheet*, mimeographed, January 20, 1988.

Aviation Safety Reporting System. A change in report processing procedures in 1985 may affect the comparability of FAA's pre- and post-1985 near midair collision data.

FAA near midair collision database
As shown in Table 6.5, total reports to the FAA of near midair collisions increased every year between 1983 and 1987, more than doubling over that period. In 1988, however, the number of pilot-reported near midair collisions fell by one-third from a year earlier; they fell an additional 23 percent in 1989.

The FAA classifies near midair collision reports by degree of hazard. A *critical hazard* is ". . . a situation where collision avoidance was due to chance rather than an act on the part of the pilot. Less than 100 feet of aircraft separation would be considered critical." A *potential hazard* is ". . . an incident which would probably have resulted in a collision if no action had been taken by either pilot. Closest proximity of less than 500 feet would usually be required in this case." *No hazard* is ". . . when direction and altitude would have made a midair collision improbable regardless of evasive action taken."[10] The unclassified category refers to NMAC reports where the inspector was unable to determine the hazard category. During the 1983-1989 period critical and potential hazards accounted for between 61 and 80 percent of total near midair collision reports, suggesting that a large proportion of the reports filed involved a clear risk to safety.

NASA's aviation safety reporting system data
The Aviation Safety Reporting System (ASRS) originally was set up by the FAA to accumulate information on near midair collision incidents. It was designed as a voluntary reporting system, but after concerns were raised about possible repercussions from reports, the system was transferred to NASA. The data system is presently managed by a third party contractor with no regulatory authority.

Because all ASRS reports are voluntarily submitted, there is no way to determine if the data are representative of all such incidents.[11] Also, not all members of the nation's aviation system are equally aware of or equally willing to make reports to ASRS, introducing possible reporting biases into the data set. The two

---

[10]U.S. Department of Transportation, Federal Aviation Administration, Office of Aviation Safety, Safety Analysis Division, *Selected Statistics Concerning Pilot Reported Near Midair Collisions (1983-1986)*, mimeographed, October, 1987.

[11]Battelle, Aviation Safety Reporting System Office, *An Overview of the Aviation Safety Reporting System*, November 1987.

Table 6.5 Pilot Reported Near Midair Collisions by Class of Hazard, FAA Data[a]

Year	Total	Critical		Potential		No Hazard		Unclassified	
1983	475	97	(20.4)	284	(59.8)	85	(17.9)	9	(1.9)
1984	589	127	(21.6)	317	(53.8)	115	(19.5)	30	(5.1)
1985	758	180	(23.7)	423	(55.8)	133	(17.5)	22	(2.9)
1986	840	98	(11.7)	414	(49.3)	301	(35.8)	27	(3.2)
1987	1058	111	(10.5)	540	(51.0)	383	(36.2)	24	(2.2)
1988	710	79	(11.1)	385	(54.2)	229	(32.3)	17	(2.4)
1989	549	60	(10.9)	275	(50.1)	197	(35.9)	17	(3.1)

[a]Percentage of total in parentheses.

Source: U.S. Department of Transportation, FAA, Office of Aviation Safety, Safety Analysis Division, *Selected Statistics Concerning Pilot Reported Near Midair Collisions (1983-1986)*, mimeographed, October 1987 and data derived from computer files provided by the Office of Aviation Safety; U.S. Department of Transportation, FAA, Office of the Associate Administrator for Aviation Safety, *Aviation Safety Statistics: Annual Summary Calendar Year 1989*, mimeographed, May 15, 1990.

data bases have relatively little overlap with less than 10 percent of FAA near midair collision reports found in the ASRS database.[12] Even for near midair collisions involving air carriers, only 18 percent of the FAA database were found in the ASRS data.

Reports of near midair collisions to ASRS have remained relatively stable over the 1981-1987 period (Table 6.6). Most of the NMACs were reported in terminal airspace not supervised by air traffic control radar. This overall trend is in sharp contrast to the FAA data that showed a steady upward trend during the same period. The FAA data suggest NMACs are becoming a greater problem, in absolute terms, while the NASA data suggest the absolute number of NMACs has declined since 1984.

CORRELATION WITH ACCIDENTS

The first question in assessing the value of incident data in monitoring changes in aviation safety is the correlation between

[12]U.S. Congress, Office of Technology Assessment, *Safe Skies for Tomorrow: Aviation Safety in a Competitive Environment* (Washington, D.C.: Government Printing Office, July 1988).

Table 6.6 Near Midair Collision Reports by Air Traffic Control Category, Aviation Safety Reporting System Data[a]

Year	Total NMAC Reports	Percentage of Conflict Reports (%)	Incidents in Terminal Control Airspace		Incidents in Other Terminal Airspace		Incidents Occurring En Route	
1981	434	31.7	68	(15.7)	278	(64.1)	88	(20.3)
1982	382	39.7	44	(11.5)	258	(67.5)	80	(20.9)
1983	450	38.6	60	(13.3)	301	(66.9)	89	(19.8)
1984	530	29.2	60	(11.3)	317	(59.8)	153	(28.9)
1985	526	39.0	68	(12.9)	201	(38.2)	257	(48.9)
1986	395	31.1	69	(17.5)	215	(54.4)	111	(28.1)
1987	371	28.2	61	(16.4)	215	(58.0)	95	(25.6)

[a]Percentage of total in parentheses.

Source: Data provided by Battelle Aviation Safety Reporting System Office.

the risk that appears to be indicated by the incidents and the appropriate type of accident. Air traffic control operational errors, pilot deviations, and near midair collisions all appear to be indicators of risk of midair collision.

Operational errors do not seem closely correlated with midair collisions. Terminal airspace operational errors have essentially no correlation (a correlation coefficient of -0.03) based on the eight years of available data. ARTCC operational errors have been influenced by the introduction of the snitch patch and the controllers' adjustment to it. In the four years of the post-snitch patch era, the correlation with midair collisions is only 0.20. Over the same period, operational errors are actually negatively correlated with the FAA's count of total near midair collisions (-0.84) and critical near midair collisions (-0.83).

Because there are only five years of pilot deviation data, reliable conclusions cannot be drawn about their correlation with midair collisions. Pilot deviations resulting in a loss of separation are highly correlated over the period, but total pilot deviations, deviations that resulted in violation of restricted airspace, and deviations by general aviation pilots are negatively correlated. Five years of data are simply too little upon which to base a conclusion.

Near midair collisions are also not strongly correlated with midair collisions. Indeed, near midair collisions as reported to the ASRS show no correlation (-0.08) over the seven years of available data. Midair collisions reported to the FAA have a correlation coefficient of only 0.51, although critical NMACs are somewhat higher at 0.76. The FAA correlation is based on only seven years of data.

The poor correlation between potential midair collision incidents and accidents is disappointing to those seeking nonaccident leading indicators of aviation safety, but may not be surprising in light of the characteristics of the incident data. First, of course, the data have not been collected long enough to find a relationship even if one existed. Second, because of discretion in reporting incidents, changes in the data may reflect changes in the number of incidents or changes in the propensity to report or both. It is only a change in the number of incidents that one would expect might be related to accidents, not a change in reporting. In fact, if reporting increases due to greater awareness, an inverse relation between reports and accidents might be observed.

Finally, even if the data problems were to be solved, one would not expect a constant relationship between incidents and accidents. Improving aviation safety consists of two tasks: reducing the number of hazardous incidents and reducing the chance that a hazardous incident will end in an accident. A considerable amount of effort in the aviation industry is devoted to this second task—changing the relationship between incidents and accidents.

In the case of midair collisions, the development and eventual implementation of collision avoidance systems is specifically intended to make sure that operational errors, pilot deviations, and near midair collisions do not become midair collisions. Windshear provides another example of pursuing both tasks. There are efforts both to detect windshear conditions so that pilots can avoid them and to improve pilot training and equipment so that if windshear is encountered there is a better chance of avoiding an accident.

FAA INITIATIVES TO REDUCE NEAR MIDAIR COLLISIONS

The rise in reported operational errors and near midair collisions prompted the FAA to convene an Interagency Task Force in 1987. The task force developed seventeen recommendations, calling for enhancement of pilot proficiency; improved air traffic control service, and the adoption of collision avoidance technology.

Specifically, in 1988 the FAA added new Air Radar Service Areas, bringing the total to 125. In response to the large number of incidents in southern California, a Special Flight Rules Area was designated, creating a separate VFR corridor through the Los Angeles terminal control area. Additionally, the FAA strengthened the "Keep 'em High" program, which keeps high-performance IFR aircraft above low-altitude VFR (general aviation) traffic.

In terms of collision avoidance, the FAA initiated the TCAS II Limited Installation Program, which is aimed at installing collision tracking equipment at selected airports. Perhaps most importantly, the FAA has proposed requirements that all aircraft must have Mode C encoding transponders within forty miles of 254 airports that have approach control radar. The extension of this requirement should reduce near midair collisions by giving controllers more information to help guide traffic management.

RUNWAY INCURSIONS

Runway incursion incident data are another potential leading indicator of accidents. These data are certain to receive increased attention, especially in light of fatal accidents in late 1990 and early 1991. In Detroit in December 1990, a Northwest DC-9 mistakenly taxied onto an active runway in heavy fog and was struck by a Northwest B-727 during its takeoff roll, killing eight people in the DC-9. In January 1991, a USAir B-737 was cleared to land on a runway already occupied by a Skywest Metroliner, resulting in twenty-two deaths. Also, the worst accident in aviation history—the 1977 Tenerife accident—was a runway incursion.

A *runway incursion* is defined as ". . . any occurrence at an airport involving an aircraft, vehicle, person, or object on the ground that creates a collision hazard or results in loss of separation with an aircraft taking off, intending to takeoff, landing, or intending to land."[13] Table 6.7 separates runway incursions into three categories: surface operational errors, pilot surface deviations, and other vehicle incursions. Total runway incursions have decreased significantly since 1987, with a slight increase between 1988 and 1989. This increase is attributable to pilot surface deviations and other vehicle incursions. It should be noted that

[13]U.S. Department of Transportation, Federal Aviation Administration, Office of the Assistant Administrator for Aviation Safety, *Aviation Safety Statistics; Annual Summary Airspace Incidents Calendar Year 1989*, mimeographed, May 15, 1990.

Table 6.7 Runway Incursions by Year, 1985-1989

	Surface Operational Errors	Pilot Surface Deviations	Other Vehicle Incursions
1985	105	65	NA
1986	114	207	NA
1987	115	229	38
1988	89	66	23
1989	81	78	59

Source: U.S. Department of Transportation, FAA, Office of Aviation Safety, *National Aviation System Airspace Incidents, 1987 Summary Fact Sheet*, mimeographed, January 20, 1988; U.S. Department of Transportation, FAA, Office of the Associate Administrator for Aviation Safety, *Aviation Safety Statistics: Annual Summary Calendar Year 1989*, mimeographed, May 15, 1990.

the recent Northwest and USAir/Skywest incursions seem to have involved a pilot surface deviation and a surface operational error, respectively. As a result of these events, the FAA has focused special attention on ground control radar and on standardized, clearly-marked pavement indicators. Some airports had added additional features, such as traffic light systems, to help manage aircraft traffic at the airport.

In summary, data describing air traffic control operational errors, pilot deviations, and near midair collisions, and runway incursions have the potential to provide insight into the frequency with which hazardous incidents that could lead to midair and on-ground collisions occur. To be useful, however, the definitions of these incidents must remain the same over time; the severity of the risk posed by specific incidents must be taken into account; and the discretion in reporting incidents must be reduced to the point where the propensity to report incidents does not change over time.

No systematic pattern of correlation was found between operational errors, pilot deviations, or near midair collisions and actual midair collisions. In part, the lack of correlation may be because too little data are available and, in part, because changes in incident data are the combined result of both changes in the number of incidents and changes in the propensity to report. With improvements in incident data reporting, these data have the potential to provide insight into changes in exposure to risk in aviation. However, even when consistently reported data on these incidents are available in sufficient quantity, the relationships between incidents and accidents are likely to change as safety technology and practice are improved. Even so, incident data may eventually provide important indications of changes in exposure to some elements of risk.

FINANCIAL PERFORMANCE, GROWTH, AND MERGERS

Public discussions of the margin of safety have not been limited to incident data. Concerns have been raised quite vigorously about the effects of deregulation on industry structure and performance, with potential reductions in aviation safety. In particular, three issues seem central to these fears. The first is the impact of a carrier's financial situation on its safety performance. Second, is the impact of industry consolidation on safety. Third, is the impact of increased traffic handled through intensified hub and spoke route systems. These issues are of current concern in the United States and are becoming of increased concern in Canada and Australia as these countries' airline industries adapt to a less restrictive economic environment. As the economic regulatory environment changes in Europe and perhaps other regions of the world, they are likely to become worldwide concerns.

Financial Performance

Deteriorating or persistently poor financial performance can increase pressure for cost-cutting by carriers. Some fear that this may result in carriers devoting inadequate resources to many aspects of their operations—training, customer amenities, and maintenance. Proponents of this view like to point out that two of the recipients of large fines for maintenance violations in the late 1980s were financially troubled Eastern and Pan Am.

However, most research has found little or no support for the argument that lower profitability is associated with poorer safety performance. This paucity of evidence may be linked, at least partially, with the limited power of statistical tests that is associated with small sample sizes due to infrequent accidents. Safety outputs other than accidents are largely unobservable and difficult to measure, so most studies have tried to examine the relationship between safety inputs and such safety outcomes as accidents and fatalities.

While there has been much discussion of potential links between financial performance and safety, only a few empirical studies have been conducted. Graham and Bowes and Golbe analyzed pre-deregulation data and could find no relation between accidents and profitability.[14] An Advanced Technology, Inc., report in 1986 analyzed simple correlations between financial measures and carriers' inspection ratings in the FAA's 1984 National Air Transportation Inspection Program and found some relationship between inspection failures and airline finances.[15] However, the report fails to control for other factors that may influence ratings and thus should be interpreted with caution. McKenzie and Shugart found that airline fatalities between 1973 and 1984 have not been adversely affected by deregulation.[16] Borenstein examined stock price reactions to airline crashes and could find no evidence of a permanent decline in stock prices as a result of accidents.[17]

The most complete work to date on financial performance and safety, by Rose, argued that several market incentives encourage airlines to invest in safety.[18] First, insurance companies base premium rates for liability insurance (at least in part) on an assessment of risk providing an incentive to increase premiums for firms that increase their accident risk. Once increased premiums are taken into account, airlines may find that reducing safety expenditures would increase, rather than decrease, total costs (albeit with a lag). The effectiveness of this incentive depends upon the quality of insurance firms' information on safety levels and the linkage of insurance premiums to future risk.[19] Second, employees have strong incentives to monitor safety, particularly when linked to maintenance of equipment or to operating procedures concerning minimum equipment lists. Third, firms may have an important stake in maintaining a reputation for providing safe service in order to attract and retain business.

[14]Graham, D. R. and Bowes, M., *Do Finances Influence Airline Safety, Maintenance, and Services?* (Alexandria, VA: The Public Research Institute of the Center for Naval Analysis, 1979) and Golbe, D.L., "Safety and Profits in the Airline Industry," *Journal of Industrial Economics* 34 (3): 305-18.

[15]Advanced Technology, Inc., *An Evaluation of the Relationship Between Air Carrier Financial Condition and Safety Posture* (Washington, D.C.: Advanced Technology, Inc., 1986).

[16]McKenzie, R.B. and Shugart, W.F. III, "Has Deregulation of Air Travel Affected Air Safety?", Working Paper 101, Center for the Study of American Business, Washington University, St. Louis, 1986.

[17]Borenstein, S. and Zimmerman, M., "Market Incentives for Safe Commercial Airline Operation," mimeographed, November 1987.

[18]Rose, Nancy L., "Profitability and Product Quality: Economic Determinants of Airline Safety Performance," *Journal of Political Economy*, 98 (5) (October 1990): 944-64.

[19]Winston has examined airline insurance premiums and found that they have declined since deregulation. Clifford Winston and S. Morrison, "Air Safety, Deregulation, and Public Policy," *Brookings Review* (Winter 1988): 10-15.

Rose focuses on determining the factors associated with accidents by major carriers, including a variety of financial factors. Her research results suggested that lower operating margins are associated with higher accident levels. This result was found to be consistent across pre- and post-deregulation periods, and across samples that differentiated between new entrants and older carriers. The effect appears to be minimal for the largest trunk carriers, but may be larger for smaller jet carriers.

These research results must be viewed with caution, because some important methodological issues remain unresolved. In particular, Rose finds a statistically significant relation between accident rates and operating margins in the previous year. However, the mechanism by which this profitability-safety link emerges is not clear. For example, if carriers reduced maintenance expense in the wake of poor profits, one might expect accident rates to rise. However, there appears to be little correlation between maintenance expense per available seat mile and changes in profitability. Also, Rose's results indicate that the connection between profits and safety is only robust with respect to the smallest carriers, which do not include any of the major airlines that experienced severe financial distress in the 1980s. Finally, some concerns must be raised about the ability of one or two accidents (Air Florida and World Airways) to produce dramatically different safety rates because of their few departures.

Increased Air Traffic Volume

Air travel has grown dramatically since deregulation. The number of passengers has grown from just over 315 million in 1980 to over 500 million in 1989. The number of scheduled operations also has grown dramatically. Total air carrier operations at airports with FAA towers have increased 22 percent from 1980 to 1987.[20] Along with the expansion in hubbing strategies and the development of new hubs, concerns have been expressed that such congestion may introduce safety risks both in the air and on the ground at the nation's largest airports. The concentration of operations during connecting banks can put intense pressure on both air traffic and ground control systems. Moreover, the reliance on hub connections may increase pressure on airlines to maintain schedules.

Midair collisions do not appear to bear any systematic relationship to congestion conditions at airports, although this relationship is difficult to test because such collisions remain

---

[20]National Transportation Safety Board, unpublished data, 1988.

"rare events." The number of midair collisions have remained relatively constant since the mid-1970s. On average 88 percent of midair collisions are between two general aviation aircraft. There have been only five mid-air collisions involving scheduled U.S. air carriers between 1978 and 1984, with none in 1985, 1986, 1987, 1988, or 1989. With the continuing trend of a declining number of general aviation aircraft using congested airports during peak periods, safety risks associated with midair collisions near congested airports might be expected to continue to decline. This risk has also been reduced with the greater use of different terminal procedures and approach paths for smaller aircraft at the major hubs.

With respect to risk on the ground, there is little evidence indicating a systematic relationship between airport capacity, design features, and safety. Similarly, there do not appear to be increased numbers of terminal area taxiway incidents during busy hub connecting times.[21] Thus overall available evidence shows that despite the increase in traffic volume, safety does not appear adversely affected.

Industry Consolidation

In general, some service and market advantages accrue to airlines that have as comprehensive and ubiquitous a network as possible. After deregulation, the advantages of expansion or mergers became even more pronounced. Indeed, the wave of mergers and acquisitions has resulted in substantial consolidation in the industry. The effect these mergers will have on flight schedules and fares remains an open question. The safety implications of these acquisitions are even less clear.

There are at least three dimensions in which safety might be related to industry merger activity. First, the merging of maintenance operations and procedures is required. This necessarily involves changes in record-keeping, spare parts inventory control systems, and the like. While there is no direct evidence of the extent of these problems (every carrier reports that their merger has gone smoothly), anecdotal evidence from conversations with inspectors and others does suggest that a more vigorous oversight role may be required for FAA inspectors during the periods when carrier maintenance and control systems are being integrated.

A second potential safety issue involves the lack of standardization of cockpit design and operating procedures across

---

[21]Obviously, the fatal runway incursions that occurred in late 1990 and early 1991 require one to be circumspect.

carriers. As newly merged flight crews adjust to new cockpit designs and different operating procedures, there is the potential for increased mistakes and errors.

A third potential factor involves the merging of seniority lists among airline personnel. The older established carriers have tended to have more senior personnel, and as a result of mergers, smaller or newer airline personnel generally have been further back on the merged seniority lists. One potential effect is that flight engineers at the older carriers found themselves higher on merged seniority lists, and thus were more likely to be pushed up into co-pilot or pilot status in the larger combined system, although their recent experience levels may have been less than that of pilots coming from the smaller or newer merger partner.

An emerging safety issue of a different sort is the risk posed by an aging fleet of aircraft. Aircraft are remaining in service for longer than the engineers who designed them had anticipated. For many years, most in the aviation industry believed that with proper maintenance and inspection, an aircraft could be kept in service indefinitely. Several incidents in 1988 and 1989, however, caused aircraft manufacturers to question this long held belief. The problems and challenges of aging aircraft are addressed in the next chapter.

Chapter 7

Aging Aircraft

One of the most chilling images of recent times was the April 1988 film footage of the Aloha Airlines B-737-200 which had the top half of the front fuselage torn away in flight. While the flight crew landed the aircraft safely and only one fatality occurred, the image of passengers and crew exposed to flying debris and hurricane force winds brought concerns about aging aircraft to the fore. The Aloha plane was the second-oldest B-737-200, and had undergone 89,681 takeoff and landing cycles during its nineteen years in service.

The growing concern about aging aircraft was reinforced further by a series of incidents in 1988 and 1989. On October 5, 1988, workers stripping paint from a Continental B-737 discovered a foot-long crack in the fuselage that had been undetected by visual inspection. In December 1988, an Eastern B-727 suddenly lost pressure en route to Atlanta and had to make an emergency landing in Charleston, West Virginia. Maintenance personnel found a fourteen-inch crack in the top of the twenty-two-year-old plane. Passengers reported being able to look up and see the sky.[1] In February 1989, an eighteen-year-old United B-747, on initial climb out of Honolulu, had a cargo door fail, leading to a large section of fuselage being torn off and nine passengers being sucked out to their deaths. In July 1989, a fatigue crack twenty inches long was spotted on a preflight "walk-around" inspection of a United B-727-100 that had accumulated 46,587 landings— well below its estimated design life.

---

[1]For further discussion, see David Martindale, "How Safe the Fleet?" *Frequent Flyer*, May 1989, pp. 36-41.

In the wake of these events, unprecedented attention has been focused on the aging aircraft problem. There are four central issues. First, are some planes safer than others? Second, how safe is it to operate older planes? Third, is the aging aircraft problem a question of equipment just wearing out, or a question of inadequate inspection and maintenance? Finally, what needs to be done to reduce the likelihood of a repeat of the events of 1988 and 1989?

ARE SOME AIRPLANES SAFER THAN OTHERS?

Much of the improvement in safety performance since the 1950s has resulted from the introduction of better, more reliable aircraft into worldwide service. As Table 7.1 shows, the first generation of jet aircraft, put in service beginning in the late 1950s, had hull loss rates three to five times today's rates. The second generation of jets, which ushered in the jet age in the 1960s, resulted in a remarkable improvement in hull loss rates. Many of these plane types remain mainstays of airline fleets today, including the B-727, DC-9, and the B-737 series. At the same time, those aircraft types with higher hull loss rates, such as the Lockheed Comet, the Convair 880 and 980 series, the Caravelle, and the Trident, largely have disappeared from airline fleets, at least in the developed world.

The wide-bodied aircraft introduced beginning in the early 1970s experienced accident rates consistent with the performance of the second generation jets. Although the rate of improvement was not sustained, the industry was able to carry a much larger number of passengers for longer distances without any apparent degradation in safety. While it is too soon to tell with certainty, the latest generation of aircraft introduced in the 1980s appears on its way to maintaining or improving this safety record.

The information in Table 7.1 leads to three conclusions. First, there was a substantial improvement in jet aircraft technology from the 1950s to the 1960s. Competitive pressures, aircraft industry consolidation, and concerns about reliability have helped to push many of the older plane types with poorer accident records out of the worldwide fleet. Second, while the rate of improvement apparently has leveled off since the mid-to-late 1960s, accident rates across different types of planes are almost indistinguishable. Third, there is little evidence that the safety records of different aircraft types worsen as time passes. Table 7.1 indicates that the aggregate safety record of each plane type improved in the 1980s compared with the entire period since its

Table 7.1 Accident Rates by Type of Plane, Worldwide Commercial Jet Fleet

Service Entry Period	Plane Type	Hull Losses Per 1 Million Departures, 1959-1988	Fatal Accidents Per 1 Million Departures, 1980-1989
1958-1960	Comet 4	9.63	-
	707/720	5.11	5.03
	DC-8	5.00	3.44
	Convair 880/990	8.63	-
	Caravelle	5.58	-
1963-1969	727	0.85	0.43
	Trident	4.49	-
	VC-10	3.31	-
	BAC-111	1.83	0.63
	DC-9	1.14	a
	737-100/200	1.06	0.85
	F-28	3.90	2.83
1970-1974	747	1.90	1.26
	DC-10	2.71	1.22
	L-1011	0.90	1.05
	A-300	1.35	0.24
1981-1989	MD-80	0.78	0.38
	767	0.00	0.00
	757	0.00	0.00
	A-310/320	b	b
	BAe-746	0.00	0.00
	737-300	0.00	NA

[a]DC-9 fatal accidents are included in MD-80 figures.
[b]As of July 1989 there has been 1 A320 hull loss with approximately 4,500 A320 departures.

Source: *Aviation Week and Space Technology*, July 24, 1989, p. 60; and data compiled from Great Britain Civil Aviation Authority, *Accidents to UK Aircraft and to Large Jet and Turbo-Prop Transport Aircraft Worldwide*, London, various years.

introduction, although this difference is not statistically significant. Of course, part of this improvement results from the upgrading of earlier models of a given type, and the interaction with other safety improvements in aviation.

However, this assessment should be tempered by two considerations. First, today's aging aircraft issue is different from that faced in prior periods. In the past, major technological changes, fuel price increases, and other factors combined to accelerate retirement and scrapping of older planes. However, the continued growth in air travel has encouraged airlines to keep planes in service for much longer periods, frequently exceeding their original design lives. Because such a large percentage of today's aircraft were placed in service in the late 1960s and early 1970s, potential problems from aircraft reaching their original design lives are only now being faced. This issue has further implications, to the degree that the oldest equipment is concentrated in the hands of weaker carriers whose financial performance may preclude modernization. Internationally, the aging aircraft problem assumes an additional dimension to the extent that the oldest planes are not scrapped, but rather are sold or leased to the airlines in the developing world. This "trickle-down" effect could have the effect of putting aged, less reliable aircraft in service in the world's most difficult operating environments and in the hands of those perhaps least able to maintain the aircraft.

HOW OLD IS THE FLEET?

How "old" the aircraft fleet is depends on how "age" is measured. Jets currently in service have engineering design lives that are shown in Table 7.2. In general, flight hour design lives are more relevant for wide-bodied aircraft, given their longer average flight times. On the other hand, the number of cycles (one cycle equals one takeoff and landing) in the design life is a better measure of age for narrow-bodied planes, since they generally perform more flights but spend less time in the air on each trip. In

Table 7.2 Design Goals of U.S. Designed Jet Aircraft

Aircraft Type	Flight Hours	Number of Flights (cycles)	Number of Planes Exceeding Design Life in cycles, March 1990	
			US	Rest of World
DC-8	50,000	25,000	35	17
DC-9	30,000	40,000	407	212
DC-10	60,000	42,000	0	0
L-1011	60,000	36,000	0	0
707/720	60,000	30,000	15	117
727	60,000	60,000	8	6
737	45,000	75,000	2	0
747	60,000	20,000	1	18
757	50,000	50,000	0	0
767	50,000	50,000	0	0

Source: Winds of Change: Domestic Air Transport Since Deregulation (Washington, D.C.: Transportation Research Board, National Research Council, 1991); Aviation Data Services.

practice, because design engineers of the original jet aircraft believed the planes would be technologically obsolete after two decades, it has become customary to use twenty years as the expected life of an airplane.

As shown in Table 7.3, almost one-third of the current U.S. fleet has more than twenty years in service.[2] While the average plane was 12.7 years old in 1989, the distribution of aircraft age is strikingly bimodal. As of July 1989, almost 40 percent of the fleet had been put into service in the 1980s, as newer fuel-efficient, quieter planes were delivered. However, the strong traffic growth of the post-deregulation period also required airlines to keep planes in service longer, so that 31.5 percent of the fleet is now more than twenty years old.

The aging of the jet fleet extends beyond the borders of the United States. Table 7.4 indicates that in mid-1989, the average age of jet aircraft worldwide was 12.2 years, but that many "workhorse" aircraft like the DC-9 and the B-727 are much older. At the same time, the number of aircraft being retired each year has fallen dramatically. Boeing had forecast that between 250 and 300 older planes would be retired in 1988 alone; however, only sixty planes actually were taken out of service that year. Aviation Data Services estimates that almost two-thirds of the worldwide fleet in 1989 could be over twenty years old by the year 2000, as shown in Table 7.5.[3] If recent retirement rates continue into the mid-1990s, over half of the U.S.-manufactured jet fleet will have operated more than two decades.[4] As of late 1989, 22 percent of the world's Boeing aircraft had exceeded 75 percent of their respective design lives in cycles.[5]

The dramatic rise in orders for new aircraft in the late 1980s would seem to suggest that large-scale fleet modernization will occur in the 1990s. Aircraft manufacturers saw order backlogs in mid-1990 reach 3,100 planes with a total value approaching $120 billion.[6] This backlog is three-fourths the size of the current U.S. fleet. However, the exceptionally poor financial performance of the airline industry in 1990 and 1991, spurred by recession and

[2]The number of flight hours or cycles per aircraft was not publicly available, so it was not possible to construct flight hour or cycle-based ages for each carrier.

[3]There were 8696 turbojets in service by ICAO member airlines in 1989.

[4]In addition, these figures do not include any information as to the age of the Soviet-built fleet in operation in much of Eastern Europe, Asia, and Africa.

[5]"Higher Maintenance Standards Sought for World's Aging Fleet," *Aviation Week and Space Technology*, July 2, 1990, p. 62.

[6]John R. Meyer and John S. Strong, "An Assessment of the Airline Experience: Looking Back, Looking Ahead," *The Logistics and Transportation Review* (February 1992).

Table 7.3 Age Distribution of U.S. Airline Fleet, July 1989

Age in Years	Number of Aircraft	Percent
Under 5	891	22.6
5-10	680	17.2
10-15	578	14.7
15-20	556	14.1
20 or older	1241	31.5
Total	3946	100.0

Source: Aviation Data Services and U.S. General Accounting Office, "Aircraft Maintenance: Potential Shortage in National Aircraft Repair Capacity" (Washington, D.C.: GAO/RCED-91-14, October 1990).

Table 7.4 Average Age of U.S. Manufactured Jet Transport Aircraft in Worldwide Commercial Passenger Service, July 1989

Manufacturer	Type	Aircraft in Service	Average Age in Years
Boeing	707/720	235	21.8
	727	1682	16.3
	737-100/200	1048	11.7
	737-300/400	586	2.1
	747	685	11.1
	757	229	2.9
	767	269	3.6
McDonnell-Douglas	DC-8	279	21.6
	DC-9	848	18.2
	DC-10	369	12.8
	MD-80	617	3.5
Lockheed	L-1011	230	12.5
Average			12.2

Source: Aviation Data Services and U.S. General Accounting Office, "Aircraft Maintenance: Potential Shortage in National Aircraft Repair Capacity" (Washington, D.C.: GAO/RCED-91-14, October 1990).

Table 7.5 Jet Aircraft Exceeding Twenty Years in Service

Manufacturer	Type	1989	1995	2000
Airbus	A-300	0	20	125
Boeing	707/720	337	397	435
	727	737	1123	1647
	737	221	419	699
	747	31	265	487
British Aerospace	BAC-111	159	196	211
Fokker	F-28	10	84	144
McDonnell-Douglas	DC-8	299	342	342
	DC-9	511	745	894
	DC-10	0	202	328
	MD-80	0	0	7
All Others		135	186	219
Total		2420	3979	5538

1995 and 2000 forecasts assume no further attrition or retirement.
All Others category does not include Soviet-built jet aircraft.

Source: Aviation Week and Space Technology, July 24, 1989, p. 60.

the Persian Gulf conflict, has caused many carriers to cancel or delay their planned aircraft purchases. These financial problems raise serious doubts as to the airlines' ability to pay for new planes in the 1990s. As a result, airlines and public officials may be forced to find other solutions to the aging aircraft problem.

Even if U.S. airlines could finance new planes and accelerate fleet retirements, the problem of aging aircraft would simply be transferred elsewhere. The traditional practice is not to take U.S. planes out of worldwide service, but to sell them in the open market, creating a "trickle-down" airplane market, in which less-developed nations inherit these older planes. For example, the Boeing 707 virtually has disappeared from U.S. commercial fleets. Of the 780 B-707s produced, just under 400 remain in service.[7] While virtually all the B-707s in the developed world have been converted to private use, over 60 percent of these still are used in commercial passenger service in the Middle East, Latin America,

[7]Data on airplane fleet composition from the International Civil Aviation Organization, *Fleet and Personnel-Commercial Air Carriers,* Digest of Statistics Number 362, 1988.

or Africa. Similarly, only 65 of the 139 DC-8-50s that were made remain in use; except for a few planes in freight use or held by brokers and lessors, the DC-8-50s fly almost exclusively in Latin America and Africa. Unfortunately, the higher ongoing maintenance required to sustain airworthiness of these aged aircraft may be even more difficult for less-developed countries to finance or perform than in developed countries. From the perspective of international public policy, it is important that policies designed to reduce the age of aircraft in developed nations do not merely transfer the problem to the developing world, where they may pose a greater hazard in more difficult operating environments.

HOW RISKY ARE OLDER AIRPLANES?[8]

As reported in previous chapters, structural failures have not been an important cause of commercial airline accidents. Before the Aloha accident, most aviation industry personnel believed that, with proper maintenance and inspection, an aircraft could be kept in service indefinitely. This belief came from a combination of advances in technology and from experience. This premise was founded on the principle of "fail-safe design" adopted by the FAA and the industry in the early 1950s. In practice, this directive required that a specified level of residual strength be maintained after "complete or obvious partial failure" of a "principal structural element."

The service experience acquired by the late 1970s generally confirmed this high level of structural safety. However, a few instances of structural failures had occurred. These events, taken in combination with the recognition that economic factors would extend the desired aircraft life beyond the original design goals, led to an agreement by manufacturers, operators, and the FAA that the "fail-safe" rule should be modified to require the use of the concepts of fracture mechanics in defining the nature and timing of inspections required for continuing airworthiness certification. This new system was commonly referred to as the "damage tolerance" rule, and was put in place in October 1978. These damage tolerance provisions were added to Federal Aviation Regulations, emphasizing three elements: crack growth analysis (how fast breaks spread); residual strength analysis (at what point is the airframe unable to carry maximum loads); and inspection

[8]This section draws heavily from Chapter 5 of *Winds of Change: Domestic Air Transport Since Deregulation* (Washington: Transportation Research Board, National Research Council, 1991).

intervals and methods. The regulations then were incorporated into maintenance programs by a joint committee comprised of the FAA, aircraft manufacturers, and airlines.

The basic idea was that an ongoing maintenance program could prolong the life of a plane indefinitely. Under the old approach, structural safety was sought through redundancy, with airframe structures designed with the aim of being able to carry expected passenger and cargo loads even if airframe failures occurred. Under the new system, advances in maintenance techniques and skills led to a program that acknowledged structural degradation but attempted to manage it by ongoing inspection and repair. The underlying idea was that improvements in diagnosis and in reliability could replace redundancy as the linchpin of structural safety.

Along with the shift to a damage-tolerance philosophy, manufacturers continued to study aging aircraft. In the early 1970s Boeing undertook a major study of its B-707/720 first-generation planes. In 1986, Boeing again studied seventy-four of its oldest jets being flown by forty-three airlines in twenty-four countries. These studies, along with several others, identified and confirmed the causes of many structural problems. For example, the cold-bonding joining of fuselage panels that failed in the Aloha accident had been changed in production by Boeing in 1972. The Boeing studies also indicated that the biggest threat to airframes was corrosion, and that older planes that had undergone corrosion prevention programs during their lifetimes were less likely to fail than were younger aircraft that had not been subject to anticorrosion programs.

However, the 1988 Aloha accident resulted in a major reassessment of how to ensure the structural integrity of airplanes. Particular attention has been paid to fatigue-initiated damage. Unlike corrosion, which can be identified through inspection and then controlled before design life is reached, fatigue presents a more difficult problem. Fatigue-initiated damage increases with time, or, more precisely, with use as measured by flight hours or takeoffs and landings. Fuselage fatigue damage is caused primarily by the application of the pressurization cycle that occurs on each flight. Wing fatigue damage is caused by the ground-to-air-to-ground cycle, by pilot-induced maneuvers, and by turbulence in the air. Thus, the design life goal of flight hours is more important for analysis of wing fatigue damage than it is for the fuselage.

There are a large number of points on a plane that are susceptible to fatigue cracking; moreover, the number of locations in which cracks will begin increases with the age of the aircraft. As the number of "initiation sites" grows, there is increased difficulty in detecting such fatigue. One commonly held view is that even if such cracks were not detected, the linking up of several small cracks would be arrested by the crack "turning" at the tear straps of the fuselage or at the airframe itself.[9] This would presumably result in a safe depressurization and would allow the pilot to land the plane safely.

However, this is not the only possible scenario. If there are cracks in the tear straps themselves, or cracking in adjacent panels, then the crack may continue to spread rapidly, leading to uncontrolled depressurization and structural failure. This situation is known as multisite damage (MSD), and was central to the Aloha accident. MSD occurs when stress factors are fairly uniform, so that small cracks appear and grow at roughly the same rate. Each individual crack is difficult to see and by itself poses little problem; however, the small cracks can join together quickly to form a large crack.

The nature of fatigue-related damage also depends on the age of the aircraft. Since neither design engineering nor manufacturing is perfect, cracks occur in aircraft long before their design life is reached. This is not an aging phenomenon, but is rather an indication of where construction was deficient. In practice, these are often referred to as "local hot-spots." Some of these hotspots are revealed by fatigue tests and by the early service experience with the aircraft. As these cracks are detected and repaired, the rate of new hot-spot locations decreases with time. Experience has shown that cracking during this phase of aircraft life can be controlled to a safe level by inspection, maintenance, and repair. In contrast, once beyond design life, the airframe enters the "wear out" stage in which the frequency of cracking increases with time and where the probability of cracking over large areas is sufficient to produce an unacceptable risk of having a critical level of damage go undetected. As was shown in Table 7.2, most of the world's jet fleet had not entered this stage as of 1990, but this promises to be a growing concern in the latter part of the decade.

There is a need for a rethinking of inspection procedures. Inspection by nature is oriented toward problems that have already been identified. New occurrences or combinations of small problems easily can go undetected. As Benjamin Cosgrove, senior vice president of Boeing Commercial Airplane's engineering division, commented following the Aloha accident,

---

[9]The fuselage is constructed of panels joined together at the tear straps, similar to the attaching of drywall panels to the interior frame of a house.

Everybody was dumbfounded that it could happen. There was a sudden realization in a lot of minds that we had been saying that the aircraft gives us warning, and that was not the case [with Aloha].. . . We never expected to see the top come off an airplane. We just did not know that it could happen. It brought out that there was an issue there, and we should address it quickly.[10]

As a result, there is now more emphasis on replacement to solve structural problems. M. Richard Johnson, director of structures engineering for Boeing, states, "Multiple problems are more likely with old aircraft. This can jeopardize the failsafe concept. There are just some things you ought to fix."[11]

This philosophy was the driving force behind the FAA Aging Aircraft Forum held just weeks after the Aloha accident, and to the formation of the Aging Aircraft Task Force, an international industry group. In a departure from the past, the task force did not emphasize more frequent inspections. Instead, the emphasis was on recommending model-specific changes in maintenance programs that would require modification and replacement of structural elements, on developing programs for corrosion prevention, and on assessing the quality of aircraft inspection and repair. The task force recommended specific repairs for each aircraft type. The first set of recommendations were issued for Boeing and McDonnell-Douglas aircraft. The task force estimated that approximately 1,300 aircraft should undergo the repairs at total costs ranging between $800 million and $1.4 billion. Other independent cost estimates range from $2 billion to $3 billion.

Soon after the task force released its findings, the FAA issued an Airworthiness Directive affecting 115 Boeing planes, requiring structural modifications with a smaller estimated cost of $142 million over the succeeding four years. The new rules are linked to the age of the aircraft and to the number of cycles it has flown. For B-727s, for example, the repairs and modifications are required after 60,000 flights or twenty years; for B-737s, 75,000 flights or twenty years, and for B-747s, 20,000 flights or twenty years. The lower thresholds for B-747s are due to the fact they are involved in more transoceanic flights and coastal airports, where corrosion is likely to be a problem. All aircraft above these thresholds must make the required repairs within four years. Some critics argue

[10]Quoted in "Aging Aircraft Issue Presents Major Challenge to Industry," *Aviation Week and Space Technology*, July 24, 1989, p. 43.
[11]Quoted in "Airframe Makers Use Aging Aircraft Experience to Refine Design Practices," *Aviation Week and Space Technology*, July 24, 1989, p. 94.

that this gives the airlines too much time. They cite the February 1989 United accident in which the cargo door failure ripped open the fuselage. In that case, the FAA had previously issued a directive requiring reinforcement of cargo doors, but had given airlines three years to comply. Only after the United accident did the FAA order airlines to make such repairs within thirty days.

The work to be done on the fleet is quite extensive. For example, the Boeing proposal for B-727 aircraft urges visual and eddy-current inspection of fuselage joints and replacement of 4,150 rivets on each plane.[12] Boeing estimates that the job will take over 1400 labor hours per plane. While the FAA estimated that the B-737 repairs would cost about $900,000 per plane, industry officials believe the actual cost will be between $1.5 and $2 million per aircraft. Since many of the affected aircraft have market values in the $10 million range, such modifications may force retirements. According to American Airlines, a recent major overhaul of a B-727 cost over $800,000 in labor and materials, almost 15 percent of the value of the plane.

For some carriers, the high costs and long lead times for fleet replacement mean that modifying older planes is the only alternative. Pan Am estimated that it would have to spend $3.5 million on each of its B-747s to comply with the FAA rules. Northwest anticipates that the labor hours for heavy maintenance on its B-747s will increase 500 percent just to comply with the new directives. *Aviation Week and Space Technology* estimates that the 89 million labor hours spent on aging aircraft repairs in 1989 will more than double in the next ten years.[13]

Another major question is who will do the work. With aircraft manufacturers facing backlogs of orders for new planes, there is scarce capacity to perform such repairs and modifications. Concern also is growing about potential shortages of spare parts. Since most airline maintenance departments are fully committed to regular maintenance and inspections, the aging aircraft repairs will increasingly fall to the roughly twenty independent maintenance facilities in the United States. There also will be increasing pressure to do such work abroad. The independent portion of the maintenance industry, which represents only about 20 percent of the hangar space, appeared to have only about 10

---

[12]Eddy-current inspection involves using air currents to detect cracks in aircraft surfaces. Other inspection methods include thermal imaging, ultrasonic and acoustic analyses, and magnetic imaging.

[13]"Government, Industry Mount Major Effort to Characterize Aging Aircraft Issues,"*Aviation Week and Space Technology*, July 24, 1989, p. 65.

percent excess hangar capacity during 1990.[14] Thus, the industry's capacity may fall short of demand in order to meet the FAA's four-year goal for aging aircraft overhauls. In light of these potential demands, the FAA has acted to streamline the process of certification of foreign repair stations.

OTHER POLICY INITIATIVES

In addition to the required modifications and repairs, the FAA established an aging aircraft research and development program to run through 1991. The FAA Technical Center in Atlantic City coordinated efforts by the Transportation Department, the Defense Department, NASA, industry, and universities. Part of the effort engaged in technology transfer, to identify manufacturing, inspection, and repair techniques used in nonaviation industries. In particular, fatigue tracking, corrosion detection, and nondestructive inspection methods were studied.

NASA is also leading a nondestructive inspection research effort as part of the space shuttle program. Currently, NASA's Langley, Virginia, facility is conducting a $3.9 million nondestructive evaluation program, which studies flight loads, stress patterns and fatigue and fracture mechanics. According to both government and industry officials, several crack-detection systems are likely to emerge from the research.

However, such approaches may not yield immediate improvements in safety. As Boeing's Ben Cosgrove points out, "For the near future, we will continue to rely on a knowledgeable, trained mechanic inspecting these aircraft. About 80 percent of new structural problems are found just by trained mechanics being around the airplane. The industry must find methods of improving the mechanic's ability to find those problems."[15] Unfortunately, many of the required jobs are quite tedious and fatiguing. As Robert Goodrich, director of flight standards for the FAA, notes, "The process of having a mechanic at a hangar at two o'clock in the morning wearing 10 power [magnifying] scopes and looking at his 1,100th rivet needs some scrutiny."[16]

---

[14]For a more complete discussion, see U.S. General Accounting Office, "Aircraft Maintenance: Potential Shortage in National Aircraft Repair Capacity" (Washington, D.C.: GAO/RCED-91-14, October 1990).

[15]Quoted in "Need for International Standards on Aircraft Maintenance is Cited," *Aviation Week and Space Technology*, May 29, 1989, p. 112.

[16]*Ibid.*

However, the task of the inspector is changing. Prior efforts were directed toward finding failures after they occurred, but before they posed catastrophic risk. The new approach is aimed at monitoring elements and systems, and replacing them before they fail. Within the airlines, more emphasis will need to be placed on "early warning" signals, especially for occurrences that magnify the safety risks of other components. Similarly, government inspectors must move beyond the old approach of repeated inspections to detect structural damage.

The new approach should seek to find problems within manufacturing or maintenance processes and then develop permanent modifications that apply to more than just the one aircraft under inspection at the time. While senior FAA officials recognize this need, much inspection practice remains rooted in the past. The announced plan for the FAA to hire 900 additional inspectors by 1991 to "look over the shoulder" of airline mechanics reflects the historical orientation of "identify damage and repair it" rather than the evolving approach of "develop standards for replacement before failure occurs."

WHAT ELSE SHOULD BE DONE?

Initiatives in four areas have the potential to improve the safety of an aging aircraft fleet. First, better utilization of existing information will help establish repair and replacement standards, and will help disseminate information on incipient problems that may cut across aircraft type or manufacturer. Much effort now is directed toward simulation and analysis in demonstrating the airworthiness of new aircraft as part of the certification process. However, less attention is paid to tracking and using data from actual operating experience to resolve problems that did not appear during certification. For example, if a part is certified to have a probability of failure of 1 in a billion, but actual experience shows failure rates of 1 in 100 million, then there is often no formal feedback process to analyze the discrepancy and to suggest improvements.

Another problem involves data that are collected but not fully utilized. The FAA collects data on Service Difficulty Reports (SDRs), which report mechanical difficulties by carrier. These data have been collected for two decades; roughly 19,000 reports were filed in 1988. However, the FAA does not use this information to analyze failure patterns or to help schedule inspection efforts. While there are some problems with data quality, SDR data have potential to help establish maintenance standards and oversight.

Second, a mandatory corrosion maintenance program should be instituted. Corrosion has been a major problem with aging aircraft, comprising about 85 percent of reported structural problems.[17] To this end, the Airworthiness Assurance Task Force has proposed to abandon inspecting only a sample of planes and instead force airlines to inspect all aircraft at regular intervals.

Third, international standards for maintenance need to be established. The growth of aircraft leasing has made it easier to sell older planes and to shift planes across international borders.[18] However, maintenance regulations are drafted by individual nations and vary in toughness and enforcement. Just as in international shipping, the question of whose rules apply looms large. As Thomas McSweeny of the FAA's Aircraft Certification Office states, "If we have an aircraft in Nigeria that's sold to an operator in Peru, but it's owned by a company in a third country, who's going to be the policeman [to ensure proper maintenance]?"[19] The problem is compounded further by the fact that a lessor may not perform heavy maintenance on a leased aircraft if that maintenance can be deferred until the aircraft is returned to its owner or the next lessee. This is a growing problem as lease contracts are shifting from long-term capital leases to short-term operating leases.

Fourth, regulatory policy should be aimed at treating aircraft structures in ways similar to established practices for engines or electronic components. For example, engines are not repaired only after a problem occurs; instead, they are disassembled, inspected, and repaired on a periodic schedule. Some engine parts that could cause a catastrophic failure are "life-limited"— that is, replaced on a schedule tied to operating history. Safety policy toward airframes should move in that same direction. Research should continue on aircraft performance during extended service lives, aimed at developing standards and schedules for mandatory repairs and replacement.

Some observers have gone beyond these points to suggest that the only right answer for the aging aircraft problem is mandatory retirement for older airplanes. In an article in *Frequent*

---

[17]Reported by Jean McGrew, Douglas Aircraft director of aircraft design engineering, in "Airframe Makers Use Aging Aircraft Experience to Refine Design Practice," *Aviation Week and Space Technology*, July 24, 1989, p. 95.

[18]By the end of 1990, over 60 percent of the world airline fleet was leased; half of these leases were operating leases with terms less than five years.

[19]Quoted in James T. McKenna, "Need for International Standards on Aircraft Maintenance is Cited," *Aviation Week and Space Technology*, May 29, 1989, p. 112.

Flyer magazine, David Martindale contends that airlines face three stark choices: continue flying older planes until critical failures occur; rely on inspection and maintenance programs; or retire aircraft above a certain age.[20] He argues that the first two options will result in more structure-related accidents, some of which will prove fatal.

A mandatory retirement age, however, is a two-edged sword. Such rules create incentives to reduce maintenance in the years prior to retirement. Ben Cosgrove of Boeing believes that "If we told airlines that the airplane had to go down in nineteen years, in fifteen years maintenance would begin to drop off, and in the last two years there would be none. It would be like leased cars— it's human nature."[21]

Fortunately, there is a middle ground. Some fleet retirement will occur as a result of the fuel price increases in 1989 and 1990. Other planes will be scrapped as a result of more stringent noise regulations. For the others, rather than thinking of aircraft as single structures, it must be recognized that airframes are composed of many elements that have different lifetime and performance characteristics. This recognition leads to a philosophy of evaluating components and replacing them on a regularly scheduled basis. The more aircraft structures come to be treated like engines or electronic parts, the greater the prospects for enhancing both safety and economic performance.

[20]David Martindale, "How Safe the Fleet?" *Frequent Flyer*, May 1989, pp. 36-41.
    [21]Quoted in "Aging Aircraft Issue Presents Major Challenge to Industry," *Aviation Week and Space Technology*, July 24, 1989, p. 45.

Chapter 8

Aviation Security

The bombing of Pan Am Flight 103 over Lockerbie, Scotland, on December 21, 1988, reminded travelers throughout the world that the risk of a terrorist incident is always present and is not confined to the Middle East and other trouble spots in the world. Acts of aviation sabotage, such as hijacking and bombing, have plagued the industry for many years. However, improved media coverage of these events and closer links between political conflicts and aviation sabotage have heightened public awareness and concern.

HIJACKING

Figure 8.1 shows the number of acts of unlawful seizure and attempted seizure from 1970 to 1989 worldwide. The substantial drop in hijacking activity following 1973 can be traced largely to the institution of screening devices and metal detectors at airports. Other important factors include the international efforts that have resulted in the closing of Cuba as a safe harbor for hijackers and the growing reluctance of many nations to allow hijacked aircraft to land.

In the United States, screening procedures of passengers and their carry-on luggage have been in effect since 1973. Worldwide inspection and screening of passengers and cabin baggage went into effect July 15, 1974. The FAA reports that since that time the procedures have detected approximately 39,000 firearms in the United States and led to 17,000 associated arrests. Of course, most people detected carrying weapons at screening points had

Figure 8.1 Worldwide Acts of Seizure and Attempted Seizure, 1970-1989

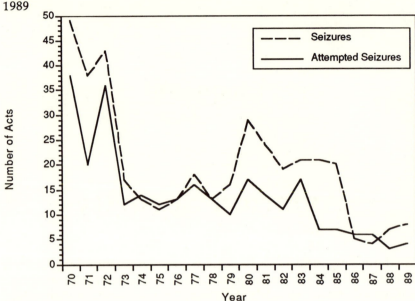

Source: International Civil Aviation Organization

no intention of hijacking a plane. However, there is little question that the security procedures have reduced the frequency of air piracy.

Hijackings that have occurred in recent years, though, are far different from those of earlier years. Now hijackings are less likely to be carried out by individuals with specific grievances. They are more likely to be the actions of organized groups that use the event itself to advance other objectives. The hijacking of TWA Flight 847 in Athens in 1986 was such a case. The Abu Nidal group held passengers hostage while seeking release of Palestinians from Israeli prisons. Also, in large part because security measures are typically tighter at U.S. airports than at many foreign airports, hijackings are more likely to occur abroad than in the United States.

Further reductions in the threat of hijacking, both in the United States and worldwide, may prove difficult to achieve. First, advances in plastics and composite materials make it increasingly likely that prospective hijackers will be able to obtain weapons that are not easily detected by conventional metal detectors and X-ray equipment. Second, even conventional weapons are not always detected by airport security personnel. In the United States, FAA tests indicate X-ray based screening systems identify test weapons only about 90 percent of the time, albeit an improvement over 1987 when a GAO study found an average detection rate of only 80 percent. For metal detectors, the FAA's regulatory standard requires an alarm two of three times a test weapon is passed through the screening device. Improved X-ray equipment has been developed, however, that could offer some hope for improved detection rates if put in service.

Third, even if screening efforts are improved substantially in the United States and at major international airports, many airports in other parts of the world are unlikely to achieve even the current level of screening performance found in the United States. While the FAA does have an ongoing program to assess the security of foreign airports, the agency does not test the operational effectiveness abroad with detection tests like those described in the previous paragraph. Basically, the FAA provides suggestions to other governments on security improvements. Also, in conjunction with the State Department Anti-Terrorism program, the U.S. government has provided other nations with security financing and equipment, including screening devices and metal detectors.

The International Civil Aviation Organization (ICAO) also places a high priority on providing financial, material, and technical assistance on security matters. Under a program established in 1990, ICAO received requests from 61 member nations, including security evaluations at 16 international airports. ICAO also has initiated development of a detailed security training program for worldwide use.

BOMBINGS AND SABOTAGE

After a sharp rise in the number of acts of sabotage in the mid-1970s, such activity leveled off in the 1980s, as shown in Figure 8.2. Unfortunately, there is a dark side to this story. Figure 8.3 shows that the number of persons killed or injured by acts of sabotage rose dramatically in the 1980s. Table 8.1 shows that the number of explosions aboard aircraft increased two and a half times from the 1960s to the 1970s. While the frequency of such acts fell in the 1980s, such explosions have become much more deadly, killing twice as many persons. More people were killed in aircraft bombings during the 1980s than in the prior 30 years combined. Table 8.2 presents a summary of recent bombings that had disastrous consequences, as well as recent missile attacks on jet aircraft. While the events in the Persian Gulf of 1990 and 1991

Figure 8.2 Worldwide Acts of Sabotage, 1970-1989

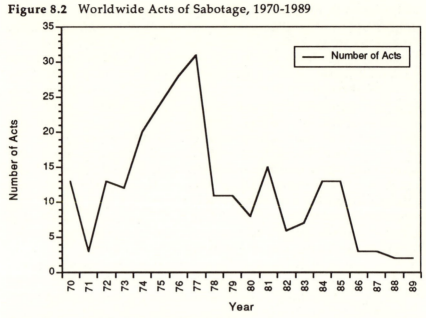

Source: International Civil Aviation Organization

Figure 8.3 Worldwide Acts of Sabotage, 1970-1989

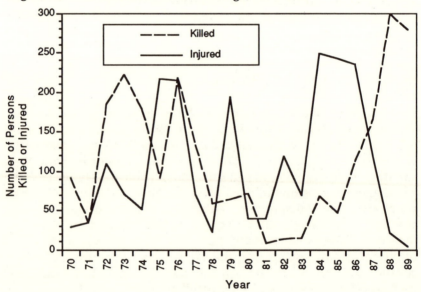

Source: International Civil Aviation Organization

146

Table 8.1 Aviation Sabotage, Explosions Aboard Aircraft, 1950-1989

Time Period	Non-Hijack Onboard Explosions	Hijack Onboard Explosions	Number of Persons Killed
1950 - 1959	8	0	62
1960 - 1969	14	1	266
1970 - 1979	28	11	650
1980 - 1989	22	3	1205

Source: Compiled from information contained in *Report of the President's Commission on Aviation Security and Terrorism* (Washington, D.C.: U.S. Government Printing Office, 1990), Appendix E.

Table 8.2 Bombings and Missile Attacks, 1983-1989

Bombings of Jet Aircraft			
Date	Airline	Location	Fatalities
9/23/83	Gulf Air	Abu Dhabi	112
6/23/85	Air India	Ireland	329
11/23/85	Egyptair	Malta	60
4/ 2/86	TWA	Greece	4
5/ 3/86	Air Lanka	Sri Lanka	16
11/29/87	Korean Air	Indian Ocean	115
3/ 1/88	BOP Air	South Africa	17
12/21/88	Pan Am	Scotland	259
9/19/89	UTA	Niger	171
11/27/89	Avianca	Colombia	107
Missile Attacks on Jet Airline Aircraft			
9/ 1/83	Korean Air	USSR	269
7/ 3/87	Iran Air	Iran	290

Source: Compiled from information contained in *Report of the President's Commission on Aviation Security and Terrorism* (Washington, D.C.: U.S. Government Printing Office, 1990), Appendix E and *Flight International*, various years.

Table 8.3 Explosions Aboard Aircraft by Region, 1950-1989

Region	1950-1973	1974-1989
North America	11	7
South America	3	2
Western Europe	8	7
Eastern Europe	1	0
Middle East	4	5
Africa	0	4
Asia	9	11
Australia/New Zealand	0	0
Totals	36	36

Hijack-related bombings are excluded.

Source: Compiled from information contained in *Report of the President's Commission on Aviation Security and Terrorism* (Washington, D.C.: U.S. Government Printing Office, 1990), Appendix E.

spurred fears of terrorist activity, Table 8.3 indicates that while much terrorism may be related to unrest in the Middle East, actual explosions, bombings, and sabotage have occurred outside that region more frequently. Thus, it is hard to escape the conclusion that while the frequency of air terrorism may have decreased, it has spread worldwide and has become much more deadly.

The probabilities of being involved in a bombing remain small. Studies of historical data indicate there is less than a one-millionth of 1 percent chance of a piece of luggage containing a bomb.[1] However, this probability may increase substantially during periods of heightened political tensions. The volume of baggage makes security a difficult task, as over 1 million pieces of baggage are checked each day in the United States alone.

The task of preventing prospective hijackers from bringing weapons aboard an aircraft seems simple and straightforward compared to the task of preventing bombs from being planted on

[1]I.M. Bar-Nir and R.L. Cole, "Coping with Bomb Threats to Civil Aviation," *ICAO Bulletin*, June 1989, p. 11-15.

planes. First, modern explosives are more difficult to detect than are firearms. Second, there are more ways an explosive device can be placed on an aircraft. Plastic explosives such as Semtex (which was used in the Lockerbie bombing) have no metal content and can be shaped to fit a wide variety of forms, including electronic components or even thin, notebook-like sheets. The manufacturing processes for plastic explosives could be modified by "tagging" explosives with additives to make them more easily detectable. In the wake of Lockerbie, the Czechoslovakian manufacturer of Semtex agreed to do so. However, enforcement of such agreements among worldwide manufacturers of similar products would be difficult. Moreover, it may already be too late, as the Czech manufacturer previously had sold 1,000 tons of "untagged" Semtex to Libya. Very little Semtex is needed to blow up an aircraft—the bomb in the Pan Am flight was concealed in a radio cassette player.

Efforts to develop detection systems for plastic explosives have focused on two principal technologies, thermal neutron activation (TNA) and vapor detection. TNA operates by bombarding baggage with neutrons, which cause the scanned items to emit gamma rays that provide evidence of specific elements and their concentration. TNA has undergone field testing of more than 40,000 luggage and cargo items and is reported to provide better than 95 percent detection ability for all types and shapes of explosives that were tested.[2]

The FAA, which invested $15 million in the development of TNA, purchased the first six units to use in U.S. international airports and one foreign airport. The first unit was installed in 1989 at John F. Kennedy Airport in New York for use by TWA in screening online and interline baggage. Another unit is scheduled to be installed at Miami and a third at London Gatwick. The FAA has identified, with the help of ICAO, a list of forty "high risk" airports where air carriers will be required to install TNA or comparable devices. Beyond the initial six units, the costs will be borne by the carriers themselves.

Several drawbacks of TNA have been acknowledged from the outset. Each TNA unit costs about $1 million and requires about six seconds to scan a single bag.[3] Because TNA equipment uses small amounts of radiation, it cannot be used for screening passengers nor is it particularly suitable for screening carry-on luggage. A more serious problem is that, despite the early

[2]*Ibid.*, p. 13.
[3]Lauren Cooper, "New Bomb Detector is Met with a Mix of Doubt, Hope," *The Wall Street Journal*, July 28, 1989, p. B1.

reported test results, these machines may not have been designed to detect appropriate amounts of plastic explosives. For example, Pan Am Flight 103 was destroyed by what most authorities agree was less than half the amount of plastic explosive material the TNA machine is expected to detect reliably.[4] When these machines are adjusted to detect smaller amounts of explosives, the rate of false alarms increases dramatically.

The President's Commission on Aviation Security and Terrorism[5] tested the machine installed at Kennedy on April 21, 1990. As the Commission reported,

> The results of the Commission's tests were startling. Although calibrated to detect the specification level set out by the FAA, the TNA machine failed to detect the explosive in two out of ten passes; it failed to detect a plastic explosive equal to 60 percent of the specification in seven out of eight passes; and it failed to detect 30 percent of the specification on any of eight passes.[6]

The Commission was so alarmed by these tests that it recommended deferral of widespread use of TNA equipment until the technology is developed further. The FAA is proceeding with demonstration testing of six TNA units, arguing that it cannot deny air travelers existing explosives detection capability while research continues on potentially better devices.[7]

Another approach, vapor detection, works by sensing the minute amounts of vapor emitted by explosives. While these systems have lower false alarm rates than does TNA, they also provide less detection ability. Also, while much cheaper than TNA (about $80,000 each), the performance is also quite slow, requiring about thirty seconds per passenger.[8] Vapor detection is thus likely to end up as a backup, complementary approach to TNA.

Even with eventual improvements in these and other technologies, the problem of preventing aircraft bombings is complicated by the variety of opportunities available to terrorists. Table 8.4 shows the location of the bomb within the aircraft for

[4]*Report of the President's Commission on Aviation Security and Terrorism* (Washington, D.C.: U.S. Government Printing Office, 1990), p. 64.

[5]The Commission was established by President Bush subsequent to the bombing of Pan Am Flight 103 over Lockerbie, Scotland.

[6]*Report of the President's Commision on Aviation Security and Terrorism* (Washington, D.C.: U.S. Government Printing Office, 1990), p. 65.

[7]Carole Shifrin, "FAA Examining New Approaches to Improve Airport Baggage Checks," *Aviation Week and Space Technology*, June 4, 1990, p. 106.

[8]James Ott, "U.S., Industry Officials Debate Funding for New Security Gear," *Aviation Week and Space Technology*, February 20, 1989, p. 118.

Table 8.4 Explosions Aboard Aircraft by Location of Bomb, 1950-1989

Location	1950-1973	1974-1989
Cabin	22	15
Baggage Compartment	4	8
Cargo Compartment	4	6
Wheel Well	2	2
Other/Unknown	4	5
Hijack Related	8	7
Totals	44	43

Source: Compiled from information contained in *Report of the President's Commission on Aviation Security and Terrorism* (Washington, D.C.: U.S. Government Printing Office, 1990), Appendix E.

nonhijack-related bombings. Even in the post-1983 period, the most common location has been in the cabin, with a substantial number also found in the baggage and the cargo compartments.

Recent public efforts have concentrated on detecting bombs contained in baggage. A particular concern is baggage checked by a passenger who does not board the flight. To guard against this possibility, U.S. carriers making international flights are required by FAA regulations to crosscheck baggage with passengers who actually board the flight. If the passenger who checked the bag is not on the flight, the baggage is taken off the plane prior to departure. Bags loaded on the plane must be checked against passengers originating at that airport as well as those making connections to the flight. For multistop flights, care must be taken to ensure that any passenger deplaning at an intermediate stop, whether ticketed to that location or not, has his or her bag removed from the luggage compartment, along with any carry-on baggage. These checks are cumbersome and can add substantially to flight delays.

A second concern is a bomb in luggage either checked or brought on board by someone who remains on the plane. Here the passenger may know of the bomb and be willing to die in the explosion or may have been unwittingly tricked into bringing a bomb on board. During the Christmas holidays in 1983, a British national unknowingly carried a bomb concealed in the lining of her suitcase from Athens to Tel Aviv to London and back to

Athens. The bomb consisted of a 1/8-inch sheet of plastic explosive concealed in the lining of the suitcase, with a triggering device containing an electronic timer and a barometric sensor. Fortunately, the bomb failed to detonate.

More recently, in April 1986, an Irish national attempted to board an El Al flight at Heathrow Airport in London unwittingly carrying a functioning bomb in a handbag. The bag had three pounds of plastic explosives concealed beneath a false bottom. The detonating mechanism was contained in a fully functioning calculator lying at the bottom of the bag. This points out another problem; hiding explosives in electronic equipment may not impair the equipment's original function, so having security personnel ask passengers to turn on a computer or radio does not remove the threat.

Advances in detection technology might eventually help locate explosives more effectively. Until that time, current detection efforts rely on individual questioning and profiles of likely bomb-carrying suspects. If an individual fits the profile, then the luggage is searched prior to boarding. On U.S. domestic flights, a passenger meeting the FAA's profile of a potential security threat has his or her luggage subjected to additional security measures. However, if the person produces an acceptable form of identification, then the baggage is accepted without X-ray. Even these limited controls are easily circumvented with curbside check-in of baggage.[9]

A third concern is cargo carried in the belly of the aircraft. Most passenger flights, both domestic and international, carry some cargo. Pan Am Flight 103, for example, carried over 20 tons of cargo ranging from electrical transformers to sewing needles to comic books. There is no obligation for a carrier to screen cargo coming from known shippers. Carriers who are suspicious of cargo may refuse to carry it, may hold it for twenty-four hours, or may inspect it. One foreign airline uses an atmospheric pressure chamber to "fly" and "land" all cargo that is to be carried on their planes.[10] While such an approach can delay the dispatch of the cargo, it offers some protection against barometric detonation devices.

A fourth concern is mail carried on flights. The U.S. Postal

[9]*Report of the President's Commission on Aviation Security and Terrorism* (Washington, D.C.: U.S. Government Printing Office, 1990), p. 48. It also should be noted that curbside baggage check-in was halted at U.S. airports during the Persian Gulf crisis of 1990-91, but was reinstated following the end of the war. Perhaps no decision better illustrates the tradeoff between aviation security precautions and reducing passenger delays.

[10]*Ibid.*, p. 64.

Service paid in excess of $1 billion to air carriers in 1989 to carry mail. No regular technological screening of domestic mail is carried out by commercial airlines. Under current law, X-ray or other screening of mail "sealed against inspection" cannot be undertaken by the airlines without first obtaining a search warrant, except in extraordinary circumstances. Typically, carriers receive mail in bound bags from the Postal Service and simply load it on the aircraft. Pan Am Flight 103 carried 43 bags of mail.

A fifth concern is a bomb placed on the aircraft while it is on the ground at the airport. Securing airport and aircraft operating areas is a major problem. Bombs can be placed in the aircraft directly or in baggage or cargo containers by an airline employee, an airport employee, the employee of companies providing such services as catering, or someone masquerading as such an employee.

SECURITY

Government regulations are the foundation for security policies and procedures, mandating that airports and airlines provide such services. In the United States, the FAA requires airports to establish a security program, to limit access to aircraft operating areas, and to provide law enforcement support. Airlines are required to adopt a security program to screen passengers and property, to provide ground and in-flight security specialists, and to prohibit unauthorized access to the airplane.

Internationally, aviation security policies are promulgated by ICAO. ICAO's standards, however, are far less strict than are those of the FAA. Indeed, a U.S. carrier operating out of a foreign airport may find the FAA standards it is required to meet are in conflict with the laws and policies of the host government.[11] This is not true in all cases, though; travelers experience much more comprehensive security checks at many European airports. Airport security provisions have been quite stringent at Japanese airports, as exemplified by the barbed wire fencing and heavily armed police at entrances to Tokyo's Narita Airport.

As the sophistication of terrorist activities has risen, so have demands on security personnel. Even in the United States, the availability of skilled security personnel is a substantial problem and it is far worse in most other countries. Most U.S. screening services are provided on a subcontractual basis to the airlines. Their personnel tend to be paid low wages, earning near minimum

[11] *Ibid.*, p. 32.

wage in some cases. High turnover occurs as a result; in some cases, turnover rates have exceeded 100 percent per year.[12] The FAA has attempted to help, doubling the number of air marshals and security inspectors since 1985. However, the government role is largely relegated to monitoring security operators.

Security services are not required to meet an established set of standards; without such requirements, enforcement actions are quite difficult. As a result, airport security efforts exhibit a strong preference for, and reliance on, technology to provide safety. However, the basic X-ray and metal screening technology widely used in airport detection systems has not changed very much since its introduction in 1973. As discussed earlier, sophisticated concealment, hard-to-detect explosives, new composite materials, and complex detonating devices reach well beyond the capabilities of the standard detection systems.

Planners of new or refurbished airports are beginning to incorporate improved security measures in their plans. Computerized access systems and closed-circuit television will be used more widely to monitor entry to secured areas. In the longer run, airports may have to separate airport and terminal functions, with passenger and baggage security checks conducted in airport holding areas physically separate from the terminal. Of course, one possible effect of this separation may be to change the locus of terrorism. The tragic attacks on the Rome and Vienna airports in 1985 raise the specter that vigilant efforts to make sure bombs do not get onto planes may result in a greater number of bombings in terminal facilities. To date, entry into terminals remains largely unmonitored worldwide. Moreover, while many airports have restricted access to gate areas and concourses, this is frequently not enforced.

NOTIFICATION OF THREATS

One issue that remains unresolved is whether governments and airlines should be required to inform passengers of bomb or terrorist threats. The U.S. Embassy in Helsinki had received a telephone message on December 5, 1988, stating that within the following two weeks an attempt would be made to bomb a Pan Am flight. No specific flight or date was named. The embassy reported the call to the FAA, which issued a notice to U.S. diplomatic

---

[12]U.S. General Accounting Office, "Aviation Security: FAA Preboard Passenger Screening Test Results," (Washington, D.C.: GAO/RCED-87-125FS, April 30, 1987).

stations in Europe and to airlines. Although some embassies notified their employees, no public announcement was made. Subsequent investigation found that this particular warning was unrelated to the actual bombing over two weeks later.

The large numbers of such threats may serve to stir unnecessary public concern, some officials say. For example, the State Department's Bureau of Diplomatic Security issued 106 messages related to terrorism in the fourth quarter of 1988, while U.S. facilities abroad received 87 telephone threats during the same period.[13]

In the wake of the Lockerbie bombing, the U.S. Department of Transportation has revised its notification system to include mandatory notice to airlines and to the pilot in command of each affected flight. The department has decided not to notify the public of all threats, on the grounds that it would compromise security sources and increase the likelihood of hoaxes. However, if threats are deemed to be "specific and credible," public announcement will be made.[14]

PROSPECTS FOR THE FUTURE

The changing nature of air terrorism and the graphic image of the Pan Am Lockerbie crash has forced governments and industry officials to confront aviation security efforts with renewed vigor. Some combination of improved technology and increased vigilance may reduce the risk from each of these concerns. However, there may be limits to the improvements such steps can make. It is likely to be far more difficult to bring security up to the highest standards in some countries than in others. Tightening security only in some regions creates incentives for terrorist activity to move to other locations. Other steps may serve more to relocate terrorism, for example, from the aircraft to the terminal, or change its form rather than to reduce it.

It is hard, though, not to be struck with how successful vigorous efforts have been with respect to specific terrorist threats. At the same time, the magnitude of the task and the time and delay costs imposed on millions of travelers also must be considered. Finally, the nature of terrorist activity is constantly changing, making the task of controlling it more daunting.

[13]James Ott and Michael Mecham, "Increased Government Role Requested to Prevent Terrorism Against Aircraft," *Aviation Week and Space Technology*, January 2, 1989, p. 30.

[14]"Transportation Department Will Require Wider Use of Advanced Bomb Detectors," *Aviation Week and Space Technology*, April 17, 1989, p. 69.

Chapter 9

Summing Up
and Looking Ahead

PRINCIPAL CONCLUSIONS

Pre-deregulation concerns about an erosion in the high level of safety in the U.S. airline industry have not been realized during the first decade of deregulation. Jet carrier safety performance has been sharply better post-deregulation than in any comparable pre-deregulation period. Perhaps more significantly in light of concerns about competitive pressures leading to maintenance shortcuts, the rate of accidents precipitated by equipment failure has been lower following deregulation. Jet carrier accidents due to air traffic control error are also less frequent, suggesting that neither the PATCO strike nor increasing congestion has resulted in decreased safety.

Deregulation's greater reliance on commuter airlines to provide service to small communities gave rise to concerns in the early 1980s about the public safety because of the commuter industry's historically poorer safety record. However, all segments of the commuter industry have improved their safety following deregulation, with very sharp improvements in the 1986-1988 period as a new generation of commuter aircraft were put into service. Large commuters, who carry the majority of the traffic, have been consistently safer than the smaller commuters. In the 1986-1988 period, large commuters as a group actually had a slightly better safety record than the jet carrier portion of the

157

industry. Most of the improvements in commuter safety have come from reduced equipment failure, less pilot error, and fewer weather-related accidents, as might be expected from tightened safety regulations and new aircraft.

Scheduled jet and commuter service accounts for only about 12 percent of aviation fatalities, with charter service and general aviation accounting for the remaining 88 percent. Charter service is generally less safe than its scheduled counterpart, with general aviation the least safe of all. The biggest difference between the safety record of jet charter service and jet scheduled service is the larger role of equipment failure in the charter segment, perhaps because many of the charter operators use somewhat older aircraft passed down from the scheduled airlines. The biggest difference between Part 135 charter service (air taxis) and scheduled commuter service is the higher share of pilot error, probably due to less-stringent licensing requirements and less-experienced pilots among charters.

Pilot error is the principal cause of general aviation accidents. Unforced pilot error accounts for 65 percent of general aviation accidents compared to 36 percent for commuters and 11 percent for scheduled jets. Among fatal pilot error accidents, the problem generally was not an inability to maintain control of the aircraft, but more often errors in judgment in which the pilot put the aircraft in unnecessarily hazardous circumstances. Indeed, poor judgment, either before or during the flight, caused more than three times as many fatal general aviation accidents as did deficient physical flying skills. General aviation's safety record is influenced in part by its role in training beginning pilots, but the impact is less than many expect. Student pilots account for only 4 percent of general aviation fatal accidents and 11 percent of nonfatal accidents. Indeed, alcohol or drug impairment causes more fatal general aviation accidents than do student pilots.

A note of caution to this improved safety record, however, is that both jet equipment failure and especially accidents due to pilot error appeared higher in 1986-1988 than they had been in the 1979-1985 period. While this increase may be an artifact of statistical variation, it occurred during a period when industry expansion and pilot retirements pulled new pilots from the commuter industry into the scheduled jet airlines at a higher rate than in the past. To the extent that the result was lower levels of pilot experience and less filtering of less proficient pilots, there could be a risk of reduced safety.

The Canadian jet carrier accident rate generally has been worse than that for U.S. jet carriers, but still excellent by worldwide standards. Most of the differences between U.S. and Canadian safety are due to more pilot error and environment accidents in Canada. In the Canadian aviation industry, as in the United States, safety generally improves as one moves from the Canadian counterparts of general aviation to charter service to commuters and finally to scheduled jet carriers. In both countries, the share of accidents caused by pilot error declines as pilots move up the career ladder starting in general aviation for initial training, then advancing to charter service, then to commuter service, and finally to jets. In addition to increasing levels of pilot experience, a filtering process occurs where only the better pilots move on to the next level. The share of pilot error starts at about the same level for general aviation in both countries and drops as one moves up the pilot career ladder, but it drops less in Canada than it does in the United States. As might be expected given the flight environment in much of Canada, the mix of accident causes among smaller airline Canadian service is more like that found in Alaska than in the continental United States.

Worldwide fatal accident rates have declined nearly 50 percent over the past thirty years. The chance of being killed in a scheduled airline crash is better than one in 400,000. However, the improvement has not been uniform and the risk of being killed in an airplane crash varies dramatically across regions, ranging from about one in 1.5 million in North America and Western Europe to one in 100,000 in Africa. In much the same manner as in the United States and Canada, large carriers tend to have a better safety record than small carriers in virtually every region of the world. Also, throughout the regions of the world, carriers operating predominantly jet fleets have a better safety record than do carriers with mixed jet and propeller fleets. Finally, as in North America, nonscheduled (charter) jet airlines generally have a worse safety record than do their scheduled counterparts.

While analyzing aviation accidents provides valuable insights into aviation safety, accident data are poorly suited to detect emerging safety problems. Efforts to develop nonaccident indicators of safety based on events where there was some discretion in reporting have been largely disappointing because of the difficulty in distinguishing changes in the frequency of the event from changes in the propensity to report the event. It is perhaps not surprising, therefore, that there is a very poor correlation between near midair collision incidents and actual midair collisions. Also, midair collisions do not appear to bear any systematic relationship to airspace or airport congestion. Similarly, despite grave concerns about the impact of a carrier's financial troubles on safety performance, there is no strong empirical support for the argument that lower profitability is associated with more accidents.

Terrorism, both in the form of hijackings and sabotage, is a frequent concern among air travelers, particularly on international flights. Both hijackings and attempted hijackings dropped sharply after 1973 with the institution of metal weapons screening devices at airports. While the number of acts of sabotage has leveled off or declined in the 1980s, the number of people killed and injured in acts of sabotage has increased. Terrorist attacks and bombings, when they do occur, have become much more deadly. Of the 36 explosions aboard aircraft between 1974 and 1989, only five occurred in the Middle East, suggesting that terrorism has spread worldwide. Current baggage screening technology is not able to detect reliably the amount of plastic explosives sufficient to destroy an airplane. The problem is compounded by the many places on an airplane where a bomb can be placed. The Pan Am explosion over Lockerbie focused concern on bombs in luggage, but, historically, the most common location for an explosive device has been in the cabin, not in the baggage compartment. Moreover, most flights also carry both mail and cargo that is not routinely examined for explosives. The Pan Am flight, for example, carried forty-three bags of mail and over twenty tons of cargo.

An important part of the improvement in aviation safety has been a substantial improvement in jet aircraft technology since the 1950s and 1960s. Newer generations of aircraft technology have proved safer and more reliable than those they replaced. The shift first from piston-engine aircraft to turboprops and more recently to more advanced turboprops in short-haul commuter service has increased safety. Improvements also have come from advances in pilot training through the use of sophisticated flight simulators and cockpit crew coordination training programs. Similarly, hazardous weather detection capability has improved; this information is being communicated to flight crews more effectively than it was in the past.

There is little evidence that the safety record of a particular aircraft type worsens as time passes. However, an older aircraft may require more careful maintenance attention than it did when it was newer. The jet airline industry is entering an era where it is flying aircraft much longer than the aircraft designers had originally envisioned, further increasing the need for sophisticated inspection and maintenance. The traditional "trickle-down" practice of carriers in the developed world passing used aircraft to the developing world has the effect of putting earlier-generation, less reliable aircraft in service in the world's most difficult operating environments and in the hands of carriers perhaps least able to maintain the aircraft. The problem of aging aircraft may become much less a problem in the developed world than in the developing one.

This filtering or passing down process is a useful frame of reference for thinking about many aspects of aviation safety. The aircraft operating in these less-safe segments of the worldwide aviation industry are typically less capable than are those in the safer segments. In the United States, for example, there seems to be a hierarchy of aircraft capability. General aviation aircraft are designed to meet the least demanding standards and typically have less redundancy and the fewest backup systems. Similarly, the aircraft used by Part 135 air taxis and charter cargo carriers are typically less capable than are those used by their scheduled commuter counterparts. Many of the aircraft used by commuters do not meet the same standards as those required of jet aircraft. Indeed, as newer turboprops meeting stricter standards were put in service in the late 1980s, the safety performance of the commuter industry improved.

While the jet charter portion of the passenger industry flies aircraft meeting the same regulatory standards as their scheduled counterparts, they often fly older models of aircraft that do not incorporate the latest technology. Many of their aircraft have seen considerable service and have reached the stage of their service lives where inspection and maintenance needs are greater. Much of the equipment flown by U.S. charter jet operators is passed down from scheduled carriers. This "filtering" phenomenon is even more pronounced among carriers in the developing world. Many of the aircraft flown in these regions are B-707s and early DC-8s that no longer are found in passenger service in the United States. Perhaps, then, it should not be surprising that a greater share of their accidents were found to have been initiated by equipment failure than for the scheduled jet carriers. Moreover, in developing countries, pilots flying older model aircraft frequently do not have the benefit of the latest technology simulators or flight crew training techniques.

Throughout much of the world, the result is a troubling mismatch of needs and capabilities. As discussed in Chapter 7, older aircraft require more extensive maintenance with more sophisticated inspection techniques to ensure their structural integrity. The ability to use these techniques and conduct the proper repairs may be most difficult to find in developing countries where it is needed most. If airlines in the developed world fly their aircraft longer before selling them to airlines in developing countries, it only transfers the problem.

Aircraft differences, however, do not explain all of the differences in safety performance among regions of the world. Many of the airlines operating in regions with relatively poor safety records operate fleets with the same types of aircraft that comprise fleets in regions with excellent safety records.[1] Thus, one must also look to differences in pilot and crew training, maintenance, weather forecasting, airports and airways, and terrorist activity.

PROSPECTS FOR SAFER SKIES

These regional and industry segment differences have important implications for the prospect of a continued trend of improved safety. The historical rate of improvement has slowed in recent years and may continue to slow. First of all, as airline accidents become increasingly rare, it becomes increasingly difficult to make further reductions in their frequency. More importantly, the pace of safety-enhancing technological innovation in jet aircraft and the rate at which technical changes spread through the worldwide jet fleet may be slowing. It remains to be seen whether growing use of fly-by-wire flight control systems, composite materials, or collision avoidance systems will produce safety improvements or enhanced reliability on the scale their proponents contend. Even if they do, it would take many years before aircraft with these innovations replace the existing worldwide fleet.

Safety improvements are often a byproduct of technological changes, rather than a direct result. Efforts at innovation are focused heavily on reducing production costs. For the manufacturers this need leads to an emphasis on production process improvement—the delivery of aircraft that have operating and capital costs as low as possible. While many might disagree, there is much less of a push for the next great leap in aircraft or air traffic control technology. This is perhaps best illustrated with the cancellation of much of the research and development related to the unducted fan jet engine, which was originally to power the MD-11. Another example is that the entry of Airbus into the aircraft market raised the technological ante, and induced a wave of aircraft improvements. However, Airbus has begun to focus on filling out its product line and placing more emphasis on commercial

[1]One exception may be Eastern Europe where carriers operating Soviet-built aircraft appear to have higher rates of engine and equipment failure.

performance rather than new product development. Whether the spate of manufacturers beginning to develop small jets worldwide will lead to a similar technological cycle remains to be seen, but with so many orders on the books, the basic aircraft technology of today will remain the standard into the next century.

It is also unfortunate that keeping air travel safe is a job replete with boring tasks. Inspecting 2000 rivets on a fuselage, screening baggage on television monitors for hours for minimum wage, and the slack periods in ATC centers where errors have occurred most often are the types of "human factors" problems that mean that technology must be relied upon for help. This creates an uneasiness among both industry officials and the traveling public—from "your flight in their hands" to "your flight in some computer's silicon chip." The tough call always has been when the systems should be allowed to work, and when human judgment should be allowed to overrule the system.

The cumulative effect of recent technological progress may require a changing perspective on many established tenets about aviation safety. The increasing sophistication of avionics software and interdependencies of flight control systems will shift the focus from testing and evaluation of single components to conducting systems evaluation and assessing the degree to which common failures can cascade through a network. New technologies bring new problems of understanding how systems can fail. Although much progress has been made, the aircraft and ATC industries still are struggling with how to validate software and how to test interdependent systems.

Another legacy of recent technology developments is a shift in emphasis from redundancy to reliability. While the industry has always sought to make components more reliable and longer-lived, these efforts were buttressed by a philosophy of redundancy. Throughout most of aviation's history, aircraft have been designed with the recognition that the failure of mechanical or electrical components was an inherent part of flying. The response was to provide back-up systems or procedures to turn to in the event of component failure. For example, multiple mechanical systems have been provided to move flight control surfaces. However, research and development efforts have produced aircraft components that now have startling levels of reliability. With these improvements, the role of some costly, performance-reducing redundancy has been called into question. Two examples of this change in philosophy are the permission given to fly twin-engine planes on transoceanic flights and the certification of the Airbus A-320 based solely on electronic flight control systems.

TECHNOLOGY AND SAFETY REGULATION

The growing importance of aircraft systems and an incipient shift from a redundancy to a reliability orientation have critical implications for maintenance and for public policy toward safety. In the past, most components would exhibit some signs of wear or diminished performance prior to posing a safety problem. Traditionally, regulatory approaches have been aimed at inspecting mechanical systems for deterioration and at identifying problems early so they can be repaired. Many components still exhibit these characteristics. However, an increasing number of new technologies are not the sort that wear out with progressively diminishing performance over time; instead, they operate at full capacity and then fail suddenly. Thus, an increasing amount of aircraft and aerospace equipment may not be well-served by an "inspect and repair" philosophy. Rather, the advent of ultrareliable electronics and other technologies requires a change from "repair when required" to replacement on a regular schedule. This change will make it easier and less disruptive for airlines to perform maintenance because such replacement can be integrated into flight schedules. However, it also requires increased vigilance on the part of regulatory authorities because deferral of such "precautionary" replacement activity is easier than it was under the old "inspect and repair" approach and, thus, may be more tempting to airlines.

The role of safety regulatory activity must continue to extend beyond maintenance oversight. Government regulatory authorities must develop and expand their technical skills in evaluating new technologies while developing new approaches to safety oversight. As aircraft and operating practices become more sophisticated, regulators will have to keep pace. At the highest levels, governments must strive to get away from a "flavor of the month" approach to safety issues. Historically, there has been a tendency to focus on a single problem, often in response to a single accident. The late 1980s and early 1990s have seen attention focused on aging aircraft, structural failure, and on bomb security. While these efforts certainly provided benefits and have made the skies safer, they tend to focus narrowly on one aspect of safety during a period in which the interdependencies among different safety factors are growing. They also tend to lead to short-term bursts of investment to "fix the problem," but then fail to ensure that the improvement is sustained.

Reducing the risk of air travel will require more than just building better aircraft and training better pilots and mechanics.

The changing nature of terrorism has forced governments and industry officials to confront very difficult aviation security problems. Better methods of detecting explosives and increased vigilance in airports may reduce the risk from terrorism. However, there may be limits to the improvements derived from such steps. It is likely to be far more difficult in some countries than in others to bring security up to the highest standards. Tightening security only in some regions simply creates incentives for terrorist activity to shift to other locations. Moreover, were the steps currently taken at the most secure airports extended to other airports of the world, determined terrorists could still pose serious threats to air travel. There are many ways to get a bomb on a plane: baggage; mail; cargo; by passengers willing to sacrifice themselves; by passengers unwittingly duped to bringing a bomb on board; by airport and airline employees; and by people masquerading as those employees. Moreover, even if the planes themselves could be made secure, airports and terminals could prove inviting targets.

As the international deregulation of airline activity continues around the world and as governments continue to divest their flag carriers through privatization, the role of safety regulation will become even more important. While "safety first" remains the credo of the overwhelming majority of industry participants, economic deregulation increases the need for vigilant, effective public oversight of safety. At the same time, governments must face up to their responsibilities in providing for airports, air traffic control, and related public infrastructure that meet the world's growing travel demands while upholding the safety of flying.

If safety is to be improved worldwide, a national approach to safety regulation will not be sufficient. Investments in the developing world in ground proximity warning systems, weather equipment, air traffic control, and airport technology will almost certainly save more lives than spending billions on, say, collision avoidance systems in the developed world. The developing world may need financial assistance to improve safety, but it also needs greater access to flight crew training, simulator practice, and the like. If continued progress is to be made, improving aviation safety can no longer be the sole province or responsibility of a few governmental bodies and a handful of manufacturers.

Public policies toward aviation safety are of the utmost importance and remain the linchpin of public trust in flying. The past twenty-five years are replete with examples of regulations that have made flying safer, such as ground proximity warning devices, the tightening of commuter airline regulations concurrent with deregulation in the United States, improved windshear detection and avoidance, and the adoption of cabin flammability standards to enhance the survivability of crashes. Perhaps the best example of all is the worldwide adoption of metal detection equipment in airports, which has drastically reduced the air hijackings that occurred with alarming frequency in the late 1960s and early 1970s.

In all, the aviation safety record has been one of the remarkable achievements of the twentieth century. The industry's success is a principal reason for so much attention being focused on those very rare times an airplane crashes or something goes wrong in flight, while so relatively little attention is paid to other phenomena that cause far more death and injury. It is important not to judge the safety record by individual events, but rather to learn all that is possible from each accident and implement that knowledge as swiftly and effectively as possible. It is unconscionable when accidents happen and people die because of a delayed or inadequate response to the lessons of prior events. In a world where accidents are rare but consequences tragic, improving aviation safety may best be achieved by focusing more effort on bringing those industry segments with poor records up to the best levels—on reducing the gap between risk tiers and eliminating safety mismatches.

APPENDICES
AND GLOSSARY

Appendix A

Measures of Safety

As is clear throughout the book, there are many potential reasons for aviation accidents. Each accident has its own unique characteristics and almost all involve more than one cause. Developing measures of aviation safety is difficult because no single measure can reflect everything one would like to know. At a minimum, safety measures should reflect the likelihood that an individual passenger will be killed or seriously injured while taking an airline flight, how that likelihood varies across segments of the industry, and how that likelihood has changed over time. Such measures should also help shed some light on why safety performance varies and how it can be improved. Safety measures must combine the outcomes of exposure to risk—fatalities, injuries, and accidents—with measures of the amount of exposure to risk—takeoffs, landings, flights, and so forth—encountered during the various phases of flight.

Determining the probability of being killed on a flight is one possible approach. The measure is a conditional probability that is the product of the likelihood of a fatality-producing accident and the fatality rate (proportion of passengers killed) for that accident. There are several problems associated with constructing this conditional probability. The first difficulty encountered is that both the probability of an accident and the fatality rate depend on the type of accident. For example, one would expect to have a better chance of surviving an accident where the aircraft rolls off the end of the runway on landing than of surviving a midair collision. Recent accidents support this expectation: when a DC-10 slid off the end of the runway in Boston, there were only two fatalities; however, in the Aeromexico midair collision over

169

Los Angeles there were no survivors. While in principle the aforementioned problem could be addressed by estimating a large set of conditional probabilities based on accident type, there are potential aggregation problems since each airline accident has unique elements.

A second, more serious measurement problem is the lack of a sufficient number of accidents to make reliable estimates of the probability of each type of accident and the fatality rate for each type of accident. Fortunately, airline accidents are extremely rare events. Even if such estimates could be made, there is the further problem that neither the probability of an accident nor the fatality rate could be expected to be stable over time. The continual push for improved safety by the Federal Aviation Administration, National Transportation Safety Board, airlines, manufacturers, and others should lower these rates over time. For example, recently implemented cabin flammability standards should improve postcrash fire survivability and invalidate survivability estimates based on the experience of crashes prior to the new standards. Similarly, recent efforts to improve crash, fire, and rescue operations at airports may well have reduced the number of fatalities in the 1989 United Airlines DC-10 crash in Sioux City, Iowa.

Faced with these difficulties in constructing conditional probabilities of being killed on a flight, the most common alternative approach is to construct aggregate safety rates where data permit, with outcomes in the numerator and exposure to risk in the denominator. Potentially useful outcome measures for the numerator include passenger fatalities, serious passenger injuries, accidents resulting in passenger fatalities, and accidents resulting in serious injuries to passengers.

It is also useful to examine rates for less serious accidents because frequent noninjury accidents may portend problems that could eventually result in more severe accidents. While fatal and serious injury accidents are newsworthy and cause for immediate concern, the difference between a situation that results in a major disaster and one that leads only to a minor accident, or even no accident, is often very small. Thus, it is useful to include accidents resulting in minor injuries or no injuries as outcome measures.

Selecting the appropriate measure of exposure to risk to be used in the denominator is another important decision involved in constructing aviation safety rates. Transportation safety rates are typically based on either the distance traveled or the number of trips. While one would like a measure that permits comparison across transportation modes, the nature of risk differs across modes and makes such comparisons difficult.

For surface travel in private auto, the risk is roughly proportional to the distance traveled—a 500-mile trip poses about twice the risk of a 250-mile trip with all else being equal. Thus distance-based measures have come to dominate surface travel safety assessments. Conversely, the vast majority of airline accidents and incidents occur during takeoff or landing. Therefore, a better measure of exposure to risk in aviation would reflect the takeoffs and landings a passenger is exposed to rather than distance traveled. This suggests that aviation safety rates should employ a denominator based on aircraft departures or passenger departures rather than aircraft miles or passenger miles, because distance-based measures may be misleading in assessing the risk of accidents associated with takeoff and landing. A nonstop 1000-mile flight has no greater takeoff and landing risk than does a nonstop 500-mile flight or a nonstop 150-mile flight; all three flights involve one takeoff and one landing.

Distance-based measures are particularly inappropriate when comparing the safety performance of jet carriers and commuters. In the United States the former have an average flight length of 800 miles while the latter have an average flight length of 125 miles. It would take more than six takeoffs and landings by the average commuter to travel the same mileage covered by the average jet carrier with one takeoff and landing.[1] Thus, a passenger on a commuter carrier would have been exposed six times more than a passenger on the jet to the more risky phases of flight while a distance-based measure would consider the risk faced by both passengers to be similar. To assess properly the likelihood of a passenger being killed or injured, the aviation safety rate should be based on passenger departures rather than aircraft departures.

Unfortunately, while aircraft departure data are frequently available, data on passenger departures are not. Enplanement data can act as a reasonable proxy for passenger departures, with a few qualifications. A passenger is counted as an enplanement each time he or she boards a flight, but, if the flight involves multiple stops, for example an intermediate stop at a hub where the passenger does not change planes, a passenger is counted as one enplanement regardless of the number of times the plane takes off and lands with the passenger on board. Thus, for flights with intermediate stops, enplanements and passenger departures are not equal. Few data are available to assess the magnitude of this divergence. There is, however, little reason to believe that

[1]Clinton V. Oster, Jr. and C. Kurt Zorn, *Commuter Airline Safety* (Washington, D.C.: U.S. Department of Transportation, 1982).

serious systematic biases for or against any particular segment of the airline industry would be introduced by using enplanements in lieu of passenger departures.

Thus, in Chapters 2, 3, and 4, where the focus is on aviation safety in the United States and Canada, the basic safety measures used are fatalities per 1 million enplanements and fatal accidents per 100,000 aircraft departures. For foreign carriers (other than those in Canada) reliable enplanement data are not available. Thus, fatalities per 1 million enplanement measures cannot be constructed and a different approach is required. The basic measures used in Chapter 5 to evaluate risk are the number of fatal accidents per million flight departures, and the measure of the "death risk" per 1 million departures based on a measure developed by Barnett, Abraham, and Schimmel, known as the Q-statistic.[2] Q is measured as:

$$Q = \frac{\sum_{i=1}^{n} x_i}{N}$$

where N is the number of flights performed by airline i and x_i is the proportion of passengers on the ith of these flights who do not survive it. Thus, if a flight lands safely x_i equals zero.[3]

Q can be thought of as the death risk per flight; alternatively, Q times 1 million can be thought of as the odds of dying in 1 million flights, which is a measure roughly analogous to the fatalities per 1 million enplanements measure used in Chapters 2, 3, and 4.

[2]Arnold Barnett, M. Abraham, and V. Schimmel, "Airline Safety: Some Empirical Findings," *Management Science*, 25: 1045-56. These same measures are also used in Arnold Barnett and Mary K. Higgins, "Airline Safety: The Last Decade," *Management Science* 35 (January 1989): 1-21.

[3]Statistically, a traveler choosing a flight at random has a 1/N chance of picking that airline's i^{th} flight, and a conditional probability x_i of being killed on the flight he or she has chosen.

Appendix B

Definitions and Rules for Assigning Causes to Accidents

Accidents to be categorized include only flights in fixed-wing aircraft designated in the NTSB accident data as airplanes. All accidents involving helicopters, balloons, gliders, and gyrocopters are excluded. Within the airplane category, ultralights are also excluded. Homebuilt aircraft are classified separately as described in the following.

EQUIPMENT FAILURE

Engine Failure: Engine failure includes any failure in-flight or during the takeoff roll of the power plant including propellers, internal engine parts, carburetors, exhaust systems, turbos, magnetos, fuel lines downstream of the fuel tank, engine controls, fuel contamination other than problems that should have been detected during preflight checks (water, misfueling, etc.).

    If the pilot claims that the engine failed and postcrash inspection fails to determine a cause of the engine failure, the accident is considered as an engine failure. However, if the engine runs without problem in postcrash investigation, the accident is considered as "cause ambiguous."

Instruments/ Electrical:
Instruments/Electrical includes any malfunction of aircraft instruments or any other electrical failure (other than magneto). Inaccurate fuel gauge is not considered instrument failure.

Landing Gear/ Tires:
This category includes any malfunction of the landing gear, tires, or brakes. However, it does not include malfunction from a hard landing or excessive side loads (ground loops).

Structure:
This category includes failure of wings, flight control surfaces, or other structural parts of the plane (ailerons, horizontal and vertical stabilizers, etc.).

Homebuilt:
This category includes any mechanical, structural, or electrical failure of a homebuilt aircraft. Homebuilt aircraft are identified either by being designated as a homebuilt in the accident brief or if the manufacturer's name is the same as the pilot's name.

Other:
This category includes all other equipment failures such as failure of the seat leading to a loss of control of the aircraft.

SEATBELT NOT FASTENED

This category is to be used when a passenger injury results from not having his or her seatbelt fastened when turbulence is encountered and adequate warning had been given by the flight crew. Adequate warning must include the seatbelt sign being illuminated and, if it had been previously turned off in flight, must include an announcement by a member of the flight deck crew or cabin crew.

ENVIRONMENT

Weather: This category includes accidents resulting from windshear, thunderstorm-related turbulence, slippery runway (unless the pilot lands excessively long), emergency landings due to weather, and icing. Weather encountered during takeoff is considered to be pilot error preflight judgment. If a weather briefing is not obtained prior to the flight, the cause is likely preflight judgment rather than weather. If a VFR-rated pilot encounters predicted weather beyond his or her capabilities, it is preflight judgment. Attempting to land at an airport below minimums is weather only if no alternative airport is available. Windy conditions during takeoff or landing (while airborne) that are corroborated by weather data or witnesses are considered as weather accidents. Otherwise such accidents are to be categorized as flying skills or, if high winds are known to the pilot prior to landing (takeoff) as inflight judgment error (preflight judgment error). Downdrafts in mountainous terrain are considered weather if altitude is 1000 above ground level or more at the time downdraft is encountered. Otherwise the accident is to be considered in-flight judgment.

Animals: This category includes collision with any animals in-flight or on the ground. It also includes accidents due to evasive maneuvers trying to avoid animals.

Wind Gusts: This category includes accidents resulting from encountering high wind while the aircraft is on the ground (taxi, landing roll, takeoff roll, parked).

PILOT ERROR

Flying Skills: This category includes accidents resulting from deficiencies on the part of the pilot in

maintaining physical control of the aircraft.
It includes hard landing, landing long, stalls,
becoming disoriented, and so on. Failure to
correct for a mild downdraft during landing
is considered flying skills.

**In-flight
Judgment:**
This category includes mental errors such as
failure to do landing checklist, failure to correct
for carb icing, failure to maintain proper fuel
mixture control, becoming lost, improper flap
setting for flight or landing. It also includes
errors in judgment that put the plane into a
hazardous situation such as flying at low
altitude (buzzing, hitting power lines, spotting
animals), flying into canyons, flying into rising
terrain that exceed climb capabilities of the
aircraft, choosing to land in uncertain terrain
(roads, pastures, etc.), and continuing a VFR
flight into IFR conditions.

**Preflight
Judgment:**
This category includes errors made prior to
the flight that result in an accident such as
failure to do preflight checklist, failure to get
weather briefing, takeoff for a VFR flight into
marginal weather, takeoff in adverse weather
or wind conditions, takeoff from uncertain
terrain and, starting the plane when it is
unoccupied and it isn't chocked and tied down.
Failure to detect water in fuel and misfueling
is preflight judgment. Failure to know fuel
consumption rate of the aircraft is preflight
judgment.

Fuel Management: This category includes all running out of fuel
in flight except for mechanical failures such
as leaks and/or defective fuel cells.

Student Pilot:
This category includes all pilot error accidents
by beginning student pilots up to and including
the fourth solo flight.

Homebuilt:
This category includes any pilot error accident
in a homebuilt aircraft.

Alcohol/Drug: This category includes any accident where the pilot is impaired by alcohol or drugs, including equipment failure related accidents.

AIR TRAFFIC CONTROL

En Route: This category includes accidents precipitated by errors by controllers in Air Route Traffic Control Centers (ARTCC) as well as errors by personnel at a Flight Service Station.

Terminal: This category includes accidents precipitated by errors by controllers at Terminal Area Radar Control Centers (TRACON).

Ground: This category includes accidents precipitated by errors by tower controllers.

GROUND CREW

This category includes any accidents resulting from errors by ground crew personnel including drivers of catering and fuel trucks.

OTHER AIRCRAFT

Midair Collision: Any accident when two planes collide and either of the planes are in the air. This category takes precedence over all other causes except air traffic control.

On Ground: Any accident when two moving planes collide on the ground. If a moving plane collides with a stationary plane, the moving plane is categorized as a pilot error/flying skills accident and the stationary plane uses the other aircraft/on ground category.

COMPANY OPERATIONS

Any accident resulting from systematic application of company-mandated unsafe practices.

OTHER

Aircraft Not Recovered: This category includes any accident where the aircraft was not recovered or a sufficient portion of the aircraft to allow an effective accident investigation was not recovered.

Medical Impairment: This category includes any accident where pilot error appears to have been induced by a medical impairment, such as a heart attack, and so on.

Apparent Drug Transport: This category includes any accident that occurs during the apparent transport of illegal drugs regardless of the specific cause of the accident.

No Valid License: This category includes any accident by an unlicensed pilot. A pilot whose license has only recently expired is not included in this category.

Cause Ambiguous: This category includes any accident where the accident investigation was not able to determine the sequence of events of the accident in sufficient detail to determine the cause.

Appendix C

Carriers Included in the Canadian Analysis

Level 1 Carriers
Air Canada
Canadian
Eastern Provincial
Nordair
Pacific Western
Quebecair
Wardair

Level 2 Carriers
Air BC
Air Ontario
Austin
Bradley Air
Nationair
Norcan Air
Northwest Territories
Time Air
Trans-Provincial
Worldways

Level 3 Carriers
Air Atlantic
Air Nova
Soundair
Voyager

Glossary

Accident An event that occurs when a person is aboard an aircraft with the intention of flight, or during actual flight, in which any person suffers a fatal or serious injury or in which the aircraft receives substantial damage.

ADREP The Accident/Incident Reporting System, an international database of accidents and incidents maintained by the International Civil Aviation Organization (ICAO).

Advisories FAA documents that provide guidance on aviation issues (more formally called **advisory circulars**). This term also includes bulletins issued by aircraft manufacturers to advise airlines about characteristics or features of particular planes, which may lead to potentially unsafe situations. Advisories usually contain suggested remedies, but are recommendations only; they do not carry force of law.

Aileron Control surfaces on the wings, located on the outboard trailing edge, used to control rolling (movement around the longitudinal axis).

Aircraft Owners and Pilots Association (AOPA) The principal trade association for owners and operators of general aviation aircraft.

Air Defense Identification Zone (ADIZ) Area of airspace within which the identification, location, and control of aircraft is required for U.S. national security.

Airframe The basic structure of an aircraft, excluding the engine.

Air Route Traffic Control Center (ARTCC) An FAA facility that provides air traffic control service to aircraft operating on an IFR flight plan within controlled airspace (principally during the en route phase of flight). Each ARTCC controls a specific region of airspace; control is "handed off" from one ARTCC to another when the airspace boundary is crossed. The last ARTCC on the flight path transfers control to a Terminal Area Control Center (TRACON) when the flight is about thirty miles from the arrival airport.

Air taxi An air carrier certificated in accordance with 14 CFR 135 and authorized to provide, on demand, public transportation of persons and property by aircraft.

Air Traffic Control (ATC) A service operated by the FAA to promote the safe, orderly, and expeditious flow of air traffic.

Air Transport Pilot Certification (ATP) The airline pilot licensing requirement for commercial air transport for scheduled services in the United States.

Airworthiness The certification that an air carrier has met the required standards for safety and operations and is authorized to provide aviation services.

Airworthiness directive An FAA regulation that orders certain actions to be taken by carriers, usually with regard to matters such as inspection, repairs, and so on. A directive requires mandatory action.

Altimeter Instrument that measures height above sea level or altitude.

Altitude encoding transponder A radar instrument that, upon receiving a signal, emits a return signal providing information on location and altitude.

Approach control Air traffic control service provided by a terminal area control facility. Air traffic controllers working approach control have responsibility for landing aircraft.

Aviation Safety Reporting System (ASRS) An aircraft incident database administered by Battelle under contract from NASA-Ames.

Aviation Safety Commission Presidential commission established in 1986 to make recommendations to improve the safety of the U.S. airline system.

Avionics A specialized branch of electronics pertaining to aircraft installed electronic devices, primarily used for navigation and flight control functions.

Backup Redundant system.

Bilateral agreement An international air service agreement between two nations, which specifies the level of service, authorized carriers, and other economic conditions of air transport.

Block A symbol appearing on an air traffic control display that provides information concerning an aircraft, its speed, location, and direction.

Buzz Flying at very low altitude over a particular target or location.

Civil Aeronautics Board (CAB) The U.S. agency that had jurisdiction over the development, regulation, and control of civil air carriers. The CAB went out of existence in 1984 as a direct result of the Airline Deregulation Act of 1978.

Callout The practice of verbal communication of operating procedures or checklists, generally done in the cockpit prior to departure; also, the practice of repeating air traffic control instructions.

Canadian Air Safety Board (CASB) Canadian agency responsible for accident investigation and safety recommendations; similar to the National Transportation Safety Board (NTSB) in the United States.

Carb heat Heat directed to the carburetor to prevent accumulation of ice and resulting malfunction.

Carb icing Engine malfunction caused when water becomes mixed with fuel and freezes, causing ice to accumulate.

Carburetor Engine component that supplies an internal combustion engine with vaporized fuel mixed with air.

Central Flow Control Facility (CFCF) An operating unit of the FAA that is responsible for monitoring and adjusting airborne traffic flows nationwide to reduce congestion and delays.

Certificate A document issued by the FAA to an applicant that serves as evidence that the applicant has complied with applicable statutes, rules, standards, and procedures in design, manufacturing, maintenance, or operation of aircraft.

Code of Federal Regulations (CFR) A codification of the general and permanent rules published in the Federal Register by the executive departments and agencies of the federal government.

Charter airline An air carrier that provides nonscheduled air transport services.

Checklist The sequence of procedures followed by cockpit crews in preparation for takeoff.

Civil Aviation Authority The principal aviation authority in Great Britain, similar to the Federal Aviation Administration (FAA) in the United States.

Clearance Approval given by air traffic control to undertake a certain operation, such as landing, or takeoff.

Climb The stage of flight following takeoff in which a plane ascends to cruising altitude.

Cockpit voice recorder A device that records communication and other sounds in the cockpit of an aircraft. Used to determine sequence of events in accident investigations.

Code-sharing The practice of allowing a regional or commuter airline to list its flights under the airline code of a major carrier in travel agent computer reservation systems.

Cold-bonding joint design The process, now revised, of attaching adjacent sections of aircraft fuselage together using an adhesive.

Collision avoidance system An aerospace technology that supplements air traffic control in helping avoid potential risks of other aircraft. Later versions of these systems also supply advisory information to pilots on how to avoid an impending collision or close approach.

Commuter airline An air taxi that performs at least five round trips per week between two or more points and publishes flight schedules specifying the times, days of the week, and points between which such flights are provided. Commuters are certificated in accordance with FAR Part 135 and operate aircraft with a maximum of sixty seats.

Composite materials Material used in the construction of aerospace components that is not entirely metal-based. In general, composites are different materials, such as ceramics, that are intended to provide superior strength, weight, or other features.

Connecting complex An airport facility in which aircraft are clustered to aid transfers to other flights.

Control surfaces Those parts of an aircraft that are critical in achieving or maintaining altitude, stability, and maneuverability, including ailerons, horizontal stabilizer, and vertical stabilizer.

Controller Person who operates the air traffic control system.

Cruise The stage of flight in which the aircraft has leveled out at a particular altitude and is en route to destination.

Cycle One takeoff and one landing.

Damage tolerance Engineering concept that was aimed at designing aircraft systems and components that acknowledged the probability of failure, but attempted to manage the process through ongoing inspection and repair.

Density altitude The pressure altitude corrected for nonstandard temperature.

Departure-based A method of constructing accident rates that standardizes by the number of flights, rather than by the number of passengers or the number of miles traveled.

Deplane Disembark from the aircraft.

Deregulation The process of removing economic controls, generally regarding fares, entry, and service from air transportation. In the United States, air cargo was deregulated in 1977 and passenger air service was deregulated in 1978.

Descent Moving from a higher to a lower altitude.

Downdraft Vertical wind current of much greater speed than surrounding atmosphere.

Drag The air's resistance to moving objects.

Eddy-current inspection The process of examining aircraft fuselages and structures for fatigue damage or cracking using devices that evaluate the movement of air currents over the surface.

Elevator A movable airfoil on the trailing edge of the tail of an airplane used to control climb and descent.

Encoding altimeter An instrument that provides altitude information to air traffic control.

Enplanement A measure representing the act of enplaning (boarding an airplane) by a passenger. A point-to-point flight involves one enplanement for each passenger; an itinerary including a connecting flight involves two enplanements for each passenger; and a flight that has an intermediate stop involves one enplanement for those passengers who do not deplane at the intermediate stop.

Federal Aviation Administration (FAA) The FAA is responsible for controlling the use of U.S. airspace, operating the air traffic control system, and promoting and regulating air safety and civil aviation.

Failsafe Aircraft design principle requiring that a specified level of residual strength be maintained after complete or partial failure of a main structural part; this is the basis for redundancy in the design of airplanes.

Fan jet A jet engine having a ducted fan that draws in extra air in order to provide greater thrust.

Federal Air Regulations (FAR) Basic aviation operating and safety regulations in the United States.

Fatal accident In the United States, any accident in which a person dies within thirty days of being injured.

Fixed-base operator A business that provides fuel, maintenance, and other basic flight services to general aviation, air taxis, or commercial aviation.

Flap An adjustable hinged surface along the trailing edge of a wing that increases left or both lift and drag. Used for takeoff and landing.

Flare A landing approach in which the aircraft levels out while descending, to make for a smoother landing.

Flight control surfaces Those parts of an aircraft that are critical in achieving or maintaining altitude, stability, and maneuverability, including ailerons, horizontal stabilizer, and vertical stabilizer.

Flight Service Station (FSS) An FAA-operated air traffic control facility that provides pilot briefings and en route communications and conducts VFR search and rescue services. The stations also provide weather information and other flight-related information. Selected flight service stations also provide en route flight advisory service.

Fly-by-wire Flight control technology that relies on electronic systems to control aircraft operation, in contrast with mechanical systems.

Foreign flag carrier An air carrier from another nation engaging in international air service.

Fuel exhaustion Running out of fuel.

Fuel selector The device that chooses which fuel tank to draw on.

Fuselage The central body portion of an airplane, housing passengers, crew, and cargo.

General Aviation Aviation other than military and commercial common carriage, including business flying, instructional flying, and personal flying.

Gliders A heavier-than-air aircraft whose flight does not depend upon a power-generating unit.

Ground loop Rapid spinning of an aircraft of at least 180 degrees while on the ground during a landing or takeoff roll; likely to cause damage to landing gear.

Ground proximity warning system A radar-based warning system onboard aircraft that monitors distance from terrain and provides visual notice, warning signals, and voice recommendations for evasive action. Designed to reduce accidents resulting from controlled flights into terrain.

Gyrocopters A type of aircraft that uses a gyroscope-based navigational system with helicopter-like blade propulsion system.

Hand-off The process of turning over air traffic control responsibility from one controller to another, or from one ATC center to another.

Homebuilt aircraft An airplane built from a kit or from basic material; these planes are not subject to the same standards as commercial aircraft, but are restricted as to where and when they can fly.

Horizontal stabilizer The fixed horizontal component of an aircraft's tail assembly which controls up and down movement of the tail.

Hub and spoke system A pattern of airline service that links outlying communities to a central hub airport. Hub and spoke flights are often arranged to match the collection and distribution of passengers from a number of spoke communities so that connections to cities beyond the hub are facilitated.

The International Civil Aviation Organization (ICAO) An agency of the United Nations, composed of contracting countries, whose purpose is to develop the principles and techniques of international air navigation, transport, and safety.

Icing The condition of ice forming on an aircraft's surface, particularly the edges of wings and other critical surfaces. Icing changes the aerodynamic behavior of the aircraft.

Instrument Flight Rules (IFR) Rules governing the procedures for conducting instrument flight; also a term used by pilots and controllers to indicate type of flight plan.

Incident An occurrence other than an accident associated with the operation of an aircraft that could affect the safety of operations.

Instrument-rated A pilot rating that indicates mastery of instrument operation of an aircraft. Instrument operation refers to operation of an aircraft in accordance with an IFR flight plan or an operation in which IFR separation between aircraft is provided by a terminal control facility or an air route traffic control center.

Jet An aircraft powered by an engine that produces motion as a result of the discharge of a stream of heated air and exhaust gases.

Jetway A trade name used to describe the enclosed, movable walkway that connects the cabin of an airplane with the terminal, through which passengers deplane.

"Keep-em-High" Program An FAA air traffic control initiative designed to keep high-performance IFR aircraft at higher altitudes than lower performance general aviation traffic.

Landing gear The tires, wheels and related assembly upon which an aircraft lands. In larger aircraft, the landing gear is retracted during flight.

Life-limited An engineering concept that requires replacement of a system or component after a specified period, regardless of whether the item is still operational.

Local service airlines During the regulated era in U.S. aviation, the local service carriers were a class of airlines that originally provided service to small and medium communities and which were eligible for subsidies on selected low-density routes. These carriers have since evolved into medium to large airlines. An example of a former local service carrier is USAir.

Magneto An alternator with permanent magnets used to generate current for the ignition in an internal combustion engine.

Minimal Equipment List (MEL) A checklist of aircraft items and systems, kept by each carrier, which must be operating properly for a flight to be authorized.

Minimums The lowest level of weather and related operating conditions under which specified aircraft activities can occur. For example, minimum visibility standards are required for VFR flying.

Mode C transponder A type of radar device that receives and communicates information showing an aircraft's identification, location, and altitude.

Multi-site damage Fatigue related cracking of an aircraft fuselage in which many small cracks become connected, resulting in more substantial damage.

NASA-Ames California NASA facility that has responsibility for the Aviation Safety Reporting System, a principal source of safety data, especially with respect to human factors such as pilot error.

Navigational aids Any visual or electronic device used by pilots to navigate.

Near Mid-Air Collision (NMAC) Classified by the FAA as to degree of risk; critical status is less than 100 feet separation of planes: moderate risk involves separation of less than 500 feet.

Nonscheduled service Commercial air service that does not operate on a fixed schedule, including charters and air taxis.

North American Aerospace Defense Command (NORAD) Generally refers to airspace that has restricted use due to defense or national security purposes.

National Transportation Safety Board (NTSB) The U.S. agency established in 1975 to investigate and issue recommendations to improve transportation safety. The principal accident investigation body of the U.S. government.

Operational Error Detection Program (OEDP) A program established in 1984 that automatically records violation of aircraft separation standards at air route traffic control centers.

Operational error An air traffic control event that results in violation of separation standard for aircraft, or between planes and other objects.

Part 91 The section of Federal Air Regulations that applies to general aviation aircraft.

Part 91D The section of Federal Air Regulations that applies to higher-performance general aviation aircraft, particularly corporate aviation.

Part 121 The section of Federal Air Regulations that applies to U.S. scheduled major commercial airlines.

Part 135 The section of Federal Air Regulations that applies to many U.S. scheduled regional/commuter airlines and to some air taxi services.

Professional Air Traffic Controllers Association (PATCO) The air traffic controllers labor union that voted to strike in 1981 and whose members subsequently were fired by the U.S. Department of Transportation.

Pilot deviation Pilot action that results in the violation of a Federal Air Regulation or a defense zone regulation.

Piston-engine An aircraft powered by a reciprocating internal combustion engine.

Plan view display (PVD) The computer display screen used to monitor aircraft by air traffic controllers.

Recurrent training Training programs designed to reinforce existing skills and requirements, improve, and provide new information for pilots, flight crews, ground handlers, controllers, and the aviation personnel.

Redundancy The provision of multiple systems or components designed to support the same task to provide greater safety in the event of failure.

Rotate The act of turning or raising the nose of an aircraft on the takeoff run at a speed that permits the airplane to lift off the ground and fly.

Runway incursions Any occurrence at an airport involving an aircraft, vehicle, person, or object on the ground that creates a collision hazard or results in loss of separation with an aircraft taking off, intending to takeoff, landing, or intending to land.

Service Difficulty Report (SDR) A report of equipment problems or other malfunctions that is collected by the FAA. These reports are designed to evaluate maintenance activities and to provide advance information as to potential safety hazards.

Sector A defined area of airspace, usually that under the direction of a single controller or ATC center.

Semtex An extremely powerful plastic explosive manufactured in Czechoslovakia that is believed to have been used in the bombing of Pan Am Flight 103 over Lockerbie Scotland in 1988.

Separation In air traffic control, the spacing of aircraft, either horizontal or vertical, to achieve safe and orderly movement in flight and during takeoff and landing.

Sequence initiating cause In accidents that involve multiple factors, the first event that preceded or was largely responsible for the occurrence of the other factors. Used in accident analysis to determine primary cause.

Serious injury Any injury that requires hospitalization for more than forty-eight hours, results in a bone fracture, or involves internal organs or burns.

Simulators Electronic equipment designed to reproduce characteristics of flight and potential hazards. Used in training programs to improve pilot and crew skills.

Ski-equipped Aircraft with skis used as landing gear in colder regions.

Specific point service Canadian classification of airline activity, similar to that of smaller U.S. regional/commuter carriers.

Stall The loss of lift due to excessive angle of wing to airstream or to insufficient speed of the airplane.

Tailwind Weather conditions in which the wind is blowing in the direction of travel.

Takeoff Stage of flight in which the aircraft accelerates and leaves the ground.

Taxi Movement of aircraft on taxiways, runways, or airport surface, prior to takeoff or subsequent to landing.

Taxiways Paved areas of the airport used by aircraft to proceed to or from the runways.

Terminal Control Area (TCA) Controlled airspace around a terminal within which all aircraft are subject to operating rules and pilot and equipment requirements specified in FAR Part 91.

Terminal Radar Approach Control (TRACON) A terminal air traffic control facility associated with an air traffic control tower that uses radar and air-to-ground communications to provide approach control services to aircraft arriving, departing, or transiting the airspace controlled by the facility.

Thermal Neutron Activation (TNA) Bomb detection methodology that attempts to identify explosives by bombarding baggage with neutrons and observing patterns of gamma rays emitted in response.

Tower The air traffic control facility at an airport.

Transponder A radar device that receives and transmits signal information. Used to provide information concerning aircraft to air traffic control.

Trunk airlines The original group of sixteen airlines in the United States authorized to provide domestic air service under the Civil Aeronautics Act of 1938. This group has evolved into the major airlines, including American, Continental, Delta, Northwest, TWA, and United. Pan Am generally is included in this group, although it was not part of the original set because it provided only international service in 1938.

Turbine engine An airplane propulsion system in which power is developed in a rotary engine (usually curved vanes on a spindle) that is used to drive a compressor from which thrust producing exhaust is generated.

Turbochargers A centrifugal blower driven by exhaust gas turbines, used to increase power.

Turboprop An engine or aircraft powered by a turbine driven propeller.

Turbulence Irregular wind conditions, especially characterized by strong vertical updrafts and downdrafts.

Ultralights Aircraft, usually built for one or two persons, that are made of extreme lightweight materials and powered by small engines.

Vapor detection Bomb detection methodology that attempts to find explosives by identifying vapor emissions from explosive materials.

Vertical stabilizer The upright part of an airplane's tail that helps to control yaw.

Visual flight rules (VFR) Rules that govern the procedures for conducting flight under visual conditions; the term VFR is also used in the United States to indicate weather conditions that are equal to or greater than minimum VFR requirements; in addition, it is used by pilots and controllers to indicate type of flight plan.

Walk-around inspection The visual examination of an aircraft by its crew prior to flight, to identify any problems with the aircraft.

Wide-bodied The largest category of jet aircraft, having two aisles in the cabin.

Windshear Weather phenomenon where a column of air descends rapidly and vertically to the ground where it fans out in a pattern similar to an inverted mushroom. An aircraft flying into and through windshear first encounters a strong headwind, which in itself poses no particular problem. The aircraft then encounters a strong downdraft pushing it toward the ground followed by a sudden strong tailwind that causes the aircraft to lose airspeed. This in turn creates a loss of lift causing the aircraft to descend still further to the ground. If the windshear is only moderate and if the pilot recognizes it immediately and responds properly, the aircraft may recover prior to impact with the ground. If strong windshear is encountered, recovery is not possible no matter what actions the pilot takes.

Index